Five Minutes to Success: Master the Craft of Writing

By

Jeri Fay Maynard

&

D. W. Vogel

Copyright © 2017

All rights reserved. No portion of this book may be reproduced in any form without permission from the publishers, except as permitted by U.S. copyright law.

For permissions contact:
Jeri Fay Maynard: Jeri@maynidea.com
D.W. Vogel: drwendyvogel@yahoo.com

Contents

FIVE MINUTES TO SUCCESS: 1
MASTER THE CRAFT OF WRITING 1
- FOREWORD 7
- WHY WE WROTE THIS BOOK 12
  - *A note from Wendy* 12
  - *A note from Jeri* 14
- PART 1 THE ART OF THE WRITE 17
  - *Prewriting* 18
  - *Brainstorming* 21
  - *Pantser or Plotter?* 25
  - *Scrivener* 28
  - *The Writing Habit* 31
  - *Find Your Voice* 35
- CHARACTER DEVELOPMENT 39
  - *The Basics* 39
  - *The Main Character (MC)* 43
  - *The Antagonist* 47
  - *The Sidekick* 51
  - *Internal Flaw* 55
  - *Emotional Stakes* 58
  - *The Backstory* 61
  - *Backstory: Character Arc* 63
  - *Tics, Mutterings, and Other Odd Mannerisms* 68
  - *Keeping A Story Bible* 73
- STORY DEVELOPMENT 76
  - *The Ten Word Pitch* 78

    Show, Don't Tell, and Specifics Sell 81

    Theme 84

    Does Your Theme Drive Conflict? 87

    Scene Development 90

    Narration: Who's Telling the Story? 93

    Choosing a narrator 98

PLOT DEVELOPMENT 102

    Digging Deeper 103

    Tension 108

    Conflict 111

    What Is CONFLICT and Why is it IMPORTANT? 112

    Inciting Incident 115

    Where Does Your Story Begin? 117

    External Conflict 122

    Internal Conflict = Character Growth 124

    Twists, Surprises, Red Herrings, and Reversals 126

    All Is Lost - The Darkest Day 129

    Climax 131

    Resolution 134

    The B Story 136

    The Three Act Model 139

PART 2 THE ART OF THE EDIT 143

WHAT'S NEXT? THE EDITING PROCESS 144

    The Sucky First Draft 145

    What's Next After Your First Draft is Complete? 149

    Manuscript Format 153

WHY GRAMMAR MATTERS 155

    Adverbs 159

    Adverbs of Manner 163

    Point of View 167

Head hopping *169*

The Sentence *174*

Misplaced Modifiers *178*

Subject/Verb Agreement *181*

Pronoun/Antecedent Agreement *185*

Filtering *188*

Expletives *191*

Useless Words Must Die *194*

Punctuation in Dialog *197*

Dialog *201*

Eavesdropping *206*

Dialog Tags *211*

The Dreaded Comma *216*

Comma Splice *220*

The Serial Comma *223*

Breaking the Rules *225*

The Beta Reader *228*

PART 3 THE ART OF THE SALE 233

PUBLISHING OPTIONS 234

The Overview *234*

Traditional Publishing *239*

Pros and Cons of Traditional Publishing and Why it is Important *247*

Self-publishing *255*

How to Self-publish *263*

Self-publishing Pros and Cons *267*

Small Publishers *272*

Small Publisher Pros and Cons *278*

Cover Art *281*

Submission Overview *286*

The Query Letter *293*

    The Opening Chapters 300

    Synopsis 305

    Revise and Resubmit 309

    Other Pitching Options 314

    Agents and Publishers--Where to Find Them 320

    Rejection 324

    Don't Cop Out 331

    Twitter 335

TIME TO SELL THAT BOOK! 340

    Marketing Guidelines 340

    Marketing Tools 344

    Short Stories 348

    Cons, Schools, and Other Horrifying Events 351

    Blogging for Success and Mailing List Musts 356

    Reviews: Why They Matter and How to Get Them 360

    Don't be a Jerk 365

    End Notes 368

ABOUT THE AUTHORS 371

Foreword

"Beware the Procrastination Demons" -
Brian Paone

I am celebrating my tenth-year anniversary as a published author, and on the eve of the release of my fourth novel, I realized that focus and diligence have brought me to where I am today. "Steady as she goes" can be contrived as a worn and played-out cliché, but I think it holds more weight in today's crowded market than a lot of aspiring writers give it credit for. I have been able to write (and publish) four novels through working fulltime as a police officer, having four kids (all of them are still under the age of ten), my wife being deployed to Djibouti, Africa for eight months (she's an officer in the US Navy), being in a touring band that consistently releases albums, moving to Japan for four years, being a professional copyeditor, and finding *me* time. When I am asked in interviews about how I find time to fit everything in, I joke that "sleep is for the weak," but honestly, I couldn't possibly be as prolific or productive unless I learned how to put on the blinders and stay true to course. By that I mean: minimizing bad procrastination.

There is good procrastination, and there is bad procrastination. When I think of good procrastination, I think of the artist's end result being that much more superior because they procrastinated and allowed the idea to really blossom over time. Now, don't get me wrong. Don't confuse procrastination with "spending extra time to get it right." Procrastination's little sister is the word "lazy." And yet, sometimes being lazy allows enough time to pass in the world so the world can be ready for your release. Unfortunately, this only happens about 5% of time. The other 95% of the time procrastination is evil and can kill momentum and a career faster than you can say "Crocodile Dundee for President."

So what demons will try to tempt you to taste the fruit of laziness or make excuses? First, I'd like to talk about the internet and social media. The internet (and I also mean to include social media from this point on) is a fantastic tool to help market and promote yourself after your work is released, or just prior, to retain fans or gain potential new fans, to know your book is being released. Where the internet can become a black hole of procrastination, is when someone "takes a break" to check their Facebook, or Twitter, or even their email. Social media platforms have algorithms in place, designed by some of the top programmers in the world, to subliminally try to keep you on the page. Everything from the layout to the manner in which new notifications arrive are designed to keep you put. So, I would suggest only checking your email, Facebook, Twitter etc. *after* you have finished writing for the day. If you need to take a break, do something that keeps the creative juices flowing but supplies an emotional break. Listen to a few songs, take a walk around the block, alphabetize your spice rack. Anything but falling down the rabbit hole of social media sites. Now, when I write, I keep my internet browser closed. Completely closed. Not minimized. Closed. If I need to research anything about what I am writing, I use my Google or Wikipedia app on my iPhone. That way I know I am only trapped in those functions, and I won't wander into the distraction that eventually leads to full-blown procrastination.

The second procrastination demon that I find rears its ugly head often is believing "I will get to writing today after I finish the list of A, B, and C things." If today is a Writing Day, then writing should be A on your list. When I am writing a novel, I set aside four of the seven days of the week to just writing. The other three days can be filled with cleaning the house, laundry, grocery shopping, vacuuming etc. Pick the days you are going to write … and WRITE. It's so easy to say, "Well, today I'm going to write after I start a load of laundry, vacuum the house, and go get an oil change." And what really happens is you get home from the oil change, and somehow, it's already two o'clock (probably because you spent a wasted hour on Facebook) and now it's time for the kids to come home from school. You really think you're going to get anything of quality written after the kids come home from school? No. I have four little kids, and trust me, my writing ends when that bus arrives. But guess what, if today was supposed to be a writing day, then make tomorrow the day to do laundry, vacuum, and get your oil changed. Those household tasks aren't going anywhere. Now don't misunderstand me. I hate a dirty house, dishes in the sink, laundry piled up. What I am trying to say is if today is a writing day, make it a Writing Day (proper noun). It should never be something to check off on a to-do list. Because guess what … You'll never check it off, and the procrastination demon will go to bed that night with a tummy full of victory.

***

Brian Paone was born and raised in the Salem, Massachusetts area. Brian has, thus far, published four novels: a memoir about being friends with a drug-addicted rock star, *Dreams are Unfinished Thoughts* (2007); a macabre cerebral-horror novel, *Welcome to Parkview* (2010); a time-travel romance novel, *Yours Truly, 2095*, (2015—which was nominated for a Hugo Award, though it did not make the finalists); a supernatural, crime-noir thriller, *Moonlight City Drive* (2017). Along with his four novels, Brian has published three short stories: "Outside of Heaven," which is featured in the anthology, *A Matter of Words*; "The Whaler's Dues," which is featured in the anthology, *A Journey of Words*; and "Anesthetize (or A Dream Played in Reverse on Piano Keys)," which is featured in the anthology, *A Haunting of Words*. Brian is also a vocalist and has released seven albums with his four bands: Yellow #1, Drop Kick Jesus, The Grave Machine, and Transpose. He is married to a US Naval Officer, and they have four children. Brian is also a police officer and has been working in law enforcement since

2002. He is a self-proclaimed roller coaster junkie, a New England Patriots fanatic, and his favorite color is burnt orange. For more information on all his books and music, visit www.BrianPaone.com

Why We Wrote This Book

A note from Wendy

Jeri and I know a lot of writers. Between online groups, in-person critique groups, and all the people we meet doing writing workshops at conventions, we've heard the same questions a million times.

"How do I get a book published?"

"How do I learn to edit my own work?"

"What are publishers and readers looking for?"

"Why isn't my self-published book selling?"

I love working with new writers and sharing the things I've learned about publishing. The book world is changing every day and the advice you would have received ten years ago is out of date. The answers change because there are new ways of asking the questions.

Traditional publishers. Agents. Self-publishing.

Many people have the idea that all you have to do is write a story, type "The End," and someone will show up on your doorstep with a contract and a wheelbarrow full of money. They read about "overnight" successes in the writing world and have no idea about the years of struggle that led to the "overnight" success. They don't know the answers because they didn't even know to ask the questions.

You picked this book up because you're a writer. Whether you've finished a novel or a short story, whether you never showed your manuscript to a soul or have self-published five novels to the roaring ovation of crickets, you're here because you want to learn more.

We don't pretend to have all the answers. Anyone who does is probably trying to sell you something more than just a writing book. No one has a secret formula that will guarantee bestseller status.

But over the years we've learned some things. And we'd love to share them with you.

This book is divided into sections. First, we're going to talk about story. What makes them strong or weak, how to build characters, how to know where your story really starts. Even if you've already finished your manuscript, read those sections anyway. I promise you'll learn something that will make your story stronger. Each section will teach you about some aspect of storytelling, then offer you a chance to apply what you've learned to your own writing through practice worksheets.

Next, we're going to talk about editing. No matter how you intend to get your book published, you must learn to self-edit. Even if you plan to hire a freelance editor, or you expect to land a six-figure deal with Macmillan and think they're going to do the editing for you (hint: if you can't self-edit, that's not what's going to happen), you need these skills. You'll have a chance to practice each new editing tip at the end of each section.

We'll talk about publishing… what your choices are, and how to decide what's right for you. I'll share the knowledge I gained in finding my agent and my experiences with independent publishers. Querying, submission, rejection; it's all here in gruesome detail.

We'll wrap up with marketing, and what you can do to ensure that all the work you're doing on this novel doesn't go unnoticed by the world.

No matter where you are in your writing process, you'll find advice you can use right now.

Thanks for joining us on this writing adventure. Hope to see you in print on the other side.

A note from Jeri

We were doing a Workshop called "What's Next: After You Finish Your First Draft" and realized that most of the audience wasn't ready for the content and needed a way to learn the craft.

While giving other workshops, attending Writer Critiques Groups, and being involved with online writer's groups, we noticed the same questions kept appearing. Finally, we made a list of the frequent topics and organized them into this book.

But we wanted something different. There are thousands of books about writing out there. As a lifelong educator, fascinated with how adult learners retain information, the work of William Glasser, brain based learning theories, and Robert Marzano's work, I suggested doing an interactive workbook/journal.

William Glasser, an educational theorist, claimed that:

We Learn

>10% of what we read
>
>20% of what we hear
>
>30% of what we see
>
>50% of what we see and hear
>
>70% of what we discuss
>
>80% of what we experience/do
>
>95% of what we teach

Plus, current educational brain theory says that to retain information you need to reflect on it in five-minute chunks. This means that after you learn something, the best strategy is to take time to think about the content and interact with it. This allows your brain to work like a filing system and it organizes the new content so that retrieval is easier.

That's this book. A workbook/journal with five-minute sections with an interactive piece. They can be used in any sequence, repeated, and are designed for the new writer to think about the craft of writing in relation to their own work.

It's not a comprehensive in-depth look at each topic (since books have been written about each one), but a solid introduction to the concepts and strategies. It's based on our personal experiences as well and these are techniques we use when we write or teach writing classes.

We encourage you to write, draw, scribble, illustrate, comment, and otherwise mark up the pages. Color and designs are great for helping your mind recall details later. You don't have to be a great artist. Stick figures work well. Make notes in the margins. We left plenty of white space on the page for that purpose. Comment about what works and doesn't work for you. The important thing is to engage with the content in an active manner.

Lastly, we ask you to teach those new writers around you. We've all been exactly where they are and our goal is for every serious writer to have access to the tools that will make them a master writer. We've all been taught by someone else. Keep the torch lit!

Part 1
The Art of the Write

Prewriting

There are several steps towards publishing: Prewriting, Writing, Editing and Polishing, Publishing, and Marketing. Some authors spend more time on one of these and skip others. If your current process works, then skip these pages. But if you find yourself struggling with finding ideas and developing them, Pre-writing strategies will help

Pre-writing is the stage before writing that includes coming up with the ideas and creating a plan to develop them into a complete work. Let's start with…

What if…

You're sitting on the sofa watching the cat look out the window: she quivers, and yowls. What's she watching? Most likely birds, but what if… aliens landed and scooped up the nosy neighbor lady? Or what if the mail carrier bit the dog barking at him? Or what if two squirrels rolled around in the street fighting tooth and nail as the cars had accidents while dodging them?

That's the power of "what if" for a writer. It's where the germ of a story idea comes from. Many of them will become nothing while others will bloom into a complete work.

A writer's greatest work is observing the world and asking "what if..." when something happens. Keep a list and when you are facing writer's block, pull it out and do a fast **free-write**. A Free-write is when you write for 5-10 minutes exactly what you're thinking without mentally editing yourself and then sift through it for tiny gold nuggets- ideas that have potential. (For this strategy to work, you must put your internal editor in jail and not let him/her out until the exercise is complete.). If you have time, take one of those gems and polish it up into a short blog post. If you don't, set it aside and pick it up next time you are feeling stuck.

The key isn't that you allow yourself to daydream, but that you realize the daydream time is part of the writing process.

What if… as a writer, you let your mind run unfettered and ….

Exercise: Practice Time

Make a What- if list

Now, Pick one

Exercise: *Do a Free-write on it.*

Using the What- if you selected above, time yourself.

Turn off your internal editor and write for five minutes without stopping.

Go through it with a highlighter and select the ideas with potential.

Write a 250-word piece on one of those ideas.

Brainstorming

Brainstorming is a tool used to generate as many ideas as possible in a short period of time. It's done quickly and is non-judgmental, meaning there are no bad ideas. You can use sticky notes, a large sheet of paper, or any other method of collection. One of my favorite strategies is the Bubble Map (a mind mapping tool to help you brainstorm).

Why brainstorm as an author? It keeps you from becoming stale, using the same ideas repeatedly. It expands your world and your characters. You can use it to generate both. Let's look at it for expanding a story idea. Go wild! Think outside the box! Play with ideas!!

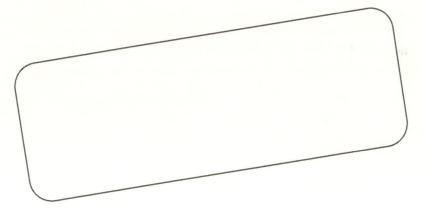

Put your "What- if" in the middle of the page and draw a circle around it. Next, jot down all your ideas, then circle them and draw a line connecting it to the what-if circle. Finish the Alien brainstorming. Pick a couple and repeat until you have the basis of a story

Figure 1: What-if Bubble Map Example

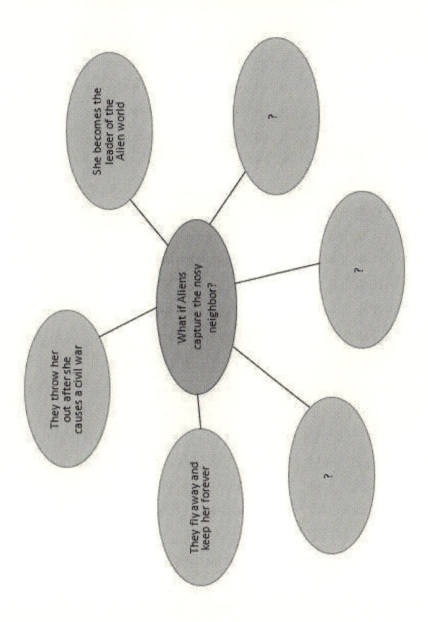

Five Minutes to Success

Exercise: Brainstorming Practice Time

Pick an idea from your "What-if" list and make a Bubble Map. After you complete one, repeat the exercise with one of the brainstorming ideas. If you like, you can circle the ideas that go together with the same color. Below the second one, write the premise in 10 words or less.

Pantser or Plotter?

What's a Pantser?

It's someone who sits down and starts to write without doing any pre-planning, writing by the seat of their pants (thus a pantser!) You start on page 1 and write until you type "the end". The good news is that doing it this way allows your creativity to flow unfettered. The bad news is that you will have to spend serious editing time fixing plotting, continuity, and tension issues.

What about the Plotter?

It's someone who plots out their work from beginning to end. You start with character development and plot steps and work through the tension to the final conflict. The good news is that when you finish the book, you may have to tweak the story structure or character growth timeline. The bad news is that you may not allow yourself to be surprised or allow your characters to take you on an exciting trip. The other issue is that you may become bored with the story and never finish it- but you'll have great notes!

The Middle Ground Writer?

Someone who does character studies, plot steps, and allows room for surprises along the way. You understand that you'll end up rewriting the beginning by the time you reach the end, but you think it's worth the energy for the feeling of adventure.

Mastering the Craft of Writing

***Exercise:* Think About It**

What kind of writer are you?

What problems does that cause you?

Is there something you can do differently?

Scrivener

How do you write? Do you sit at a desk in front of a computer? Peck away at a laptop in a coffee shop? Scribble in a notebook?

Whatever method you prefer to get your initial story on paper (or hard drive), the time will come when it needs to be in a computer file. There are plenty of word processing programs out there, and there's no reason why you can't just type your manuscript into a Word document. It's what you'll need when you start submitting it or go to upload it for publication.

But there are other choices.

Specific software exists for writers. What follows is an unsolicited promo for the software I use.

A company called Literature and Latte offers a program called Scrivener. You can get a free trial on their website, which is a full-featured program that's yours for a limited time. They hope that in that time you'll fall in love with it, and pay the $40 it currently costs to buy.

It's well worth it.

Scrivener is available for Mac or PC platforms. There's a version for your phone, too. Those of us who write on Scrivener couldn't imagine writing a novel without it.

There's a sharp learning curve. The documentation isn't great, but YouTube has lots of video tutorials which are very helpful in learning to use all of its features. It organizes your book by section (for me, that's chapters, but it can be whatever you want it to be, with subsections or without), and each section gets an "index card" on a virtual corkboard at the top. As you write each chapter, take a moment to update the index card for it. That might look like, "Chapter 3. Sally meets Ron at the Happy Times Bar and Grill. They talk about his dog. He invites her out for a late-night burger." Just enough information that you know at a glance what's in your chapter. What's amazing about this is that if you decide to rearrange your chapters later, all you have to do is drag and drop those index cards and it automatically moves the chapters for you. Think about how long that would take you in Word...copy, paste, copy, paste. This can be huge in revisions.

The other thing I love most is that you can configure it to save automatically into your Dropbox. If you don't have Dropbox, get it. It's a free cloud-based storage program. By configuring Scrivener to autosave (every single time you change a single character in the document) to Dropbox, you cannot lose your work. Even if your computer explodes mid-sentence, Dropbox has it, so when you get a new computer or switch to your laptop while you're in the burn unit having scorched computer shrapnel picked out of your forehead, your manuscript will be there. You can access it from anywhere with your Dropbox password.

It saves multiple versions, allows you to save research documents and character studies, and you can compile whatever portion you want into almost any format you can think of, including .epub and .mobi. I use this all the time. When I finish a draft, I'll compile it as a .mobi document and email it to my Kindle. Now I can read it like any e-book. This forces my brain to look at the words as if they weren't my own, and I catch mistakes I'd missed because I was so used to seeing them on my monitor.

It has a lot of other features that I don't even know how to use, and it has templates for novels, screenplays, and nonfiction.

If you love your current writing software solution, then bully for you. But if any of those features appeal to you, consider checking out Scrivener. Once you learn how to use it, you'll never write a book without it.

We now return you to our regularly scheduled programming.

The Writing Habit

Everyone does it differently. You'll see plenty of people who advise that to become a good writer, you have to write every day. Some folks get up an hour early and tap out words before the kids get up. Others write late into the night. The "write every day" crowd finds clever ways to fit the habit into their lives. Many of them fight writer's block; the dreaded blank screen and flashing cursor because some days they just can't think of what they want to say, or where they should take their story next.

I'm not one of those people. For me, if I only have an hour, that's not enough time to really get going. I write when I have a whole evening or afternoon free, which happens once or twice a week. But I think about my writing every day. When I'm out running on the trails, I'm thinking about my plot. Standing in line at the grocery I'm considering character. By the time my writing night happens, I'm raring to go, full of ideas and plans. I almost never stare at a blank screen because I've been waiting for days to write the scene that's been brewing in my mind.

That works for me. It doesn't mean that will work for you.

And it doesn't matter.

If you're a "write every day" person, then sit yourself down and write. If you're an opportunist like me, keep writing in your mind when you're not sitting in front of your keyboard.

But remember that writing takes time, and learning to write well takes a lot of time.

Lots of people put stock in the "10,000 hour rule" which says that it takes 10,000 hours of practice at something to become an expert. The key, though, is to make sure those hours are spent actually learning. Getting better. If you are a crappy tennis player and you just keep hitting the ball into the net, in 10,000 hours you'll have shoulders like The Hulk, but you still won't have any skill. If you get a coach, and maybe watch some videos, and do some practice drills, you might get better a lot faster than 10,000 hours. You might get a little better in one day if somebody shows you how to hold the racquet correctly. So make sure the hours you're putting into improving your writing are actually improving it. Read…not just books about writing, but well-written books in all genres. See if you can figure out what it is about the latest bestseller that made a million people rush to buy it. Try to sort out why a classic work of literature has stood the test of time. Make sure that what you're reading is professionally edited so you aren't picking up mistakes from other novice writers. These reading hours count toward your 10,000, and you're probably well on your way already.

Figure out what works for you. Experiment with writing at different times of day, for different lengths of time, and in different settings. I write best in my office with a cat on my lap.

Mastering the Craft of Writing

You might write best at a coffee shop, or in the park, or sitting in your car waiting to pick up your kid from soccer practice.

Whatever you do, stick with it. Try to never go more than a week without writing something. Exercise those writing muscles. Hold the racket differently. See what a new swing feels like.

Exercise: Think About It

When do you write best?

Where?

Have you ever tried changing your timing or surroundings?

What happened?

What would you like to try that's new?

Find Your Voice

Voice. We talk about voice all the time in writing. It's hard to define and hard to discuss, but you know it when you hear it.

Consider these two passages:

I am the kind of person who always succeeds. High school cheerleading captain in my junior year, sorority sister at Mason College. There was no doubt that I, Emma March, was going to succeed. I waited months to hear the verdict after my medical school interviews, and when the letter finally came I tore it open. "We regret to inform you..." Tears filled my eyes. Failure. I had never failed at anything before, and I had to start with this most important interview of my life. I tore up the letter, dumped it into a coffee mug and set it on fire. The smoke alarm blared and everyone had to evacuate the building. That was the end of my college career.

Now this one:

I don't mess around. When I want something, I go for it. Full bore, both barrels, guns a-blazin'. In high school, I was head cheerleader as a junior, and when I got to college five sororities begged me to join. Emma March gets things done. Which is why the medical school rejection letter hit me so hard. "We regret to inform you..." it began, and I crumpled it up and threw it on the tile floor of my dorm room, jumping on it until it shredded into a hundred pieces. I scooped the shreds into an old coffee mug and dropped in a match, and when the smoke alarm blared and everybody had to evacuate the building, I walked out the door and kept on walking.

Both of these passages say the same thing. They're both first person, mixed present and past tense. They both describe the same narrator and the same events. But which one grabbed you? Which one made you want to read more about Emma? Of course, it's the second one. The reason is voice.

Writing with strong voice isn't just for first person. Third can be just as powerful.

Jackson's eyes snapped open. *Oh, Lord, what have I done this time?* Face down on a cold concrete floor, his cheek was wet with drool. And his arms were chilly. And his legs. And his ass. And his...*Lord, I'm naked. Naked in...* he peered around the dimly lit room...*someone's basement?* He struggled to sit up and tried to crawl forward toward the pale outline of a doorway. Something cold and hard dug into his left ankle. He whipped around and grabbed at the cold metal chain, pulled taut against the iron ring set into the floor. *Jackson, baby, you really need to quit drinking with strangers.*

So what about that paragraph gives it voice? Partially it's the use of italicized inner monologue. Jackson's own thoughts give the scene voice. The use of the repetition (And his arms, and his legs, and his ass) also helps.

The thing about voice is that it has to be consistent. It takes time to develop, and in the early days it's easy to try and copy someone else's. You can't force it or it will feel... forced.

You might develop a singular voice that pervades all your works, or you might write in a different voice on each novel you write.

Make strong choices.

Write boldly.

Your writing voice will be what makes you unique and what sets your story apart from all the other books out there.

Exercise: Think About It

Which authors do you read whose voices are unmistakable?

What makes them so distinctive?

Character Development

The Basics

What is character development?

There are people in your story who are going on an adventure with you. They have full lives. Things happened to them before your adventure began (their backstory) and things will happen to them in the future after the story ends. They have personality, ticks, interests, peccadillos, favorites, and dislikes. They drive a certain kind of car or ride a bike because of their belief system. They have pets or hate animals. They have scars, illnesses, obsessions, or tattoos. They vote one party or the other or don't bother. They wear brand name clothing or buy at the thrift store. They love to shop or refuse to enter commercial stores. They are real-- except they exist only in your brain until you put their story on paper. While they are on this journey, they will encounter many challenges and conflicts until it affects who they are in a fundamental way and end their time with you changed, and maybe, sometimes, a better person (not always).

Why is it important?

Why do you need to know what brand of toothpaste your characters buy or why they take the bus instead of driving or why they complain about the cold when it's not that cold out? Those things make your character three dimensional and realistic. You may not use all those things, but you should know their triggers and their reactions to stress and happiness. Not every person reacts the same. Knowing how each character reacts is critical to raising the stakes to the point where the conflict is personal and driven by their choices. It's the author's job to push their buttons, let them fall apart, and pull themselves back together again. It helps if you understand how they think and why.

The Character Study

A character study is a simple reference tool to keep your characters details straight. Does Joey have blue or brown eyes? How long is Sami's hair at the beginning and when does she cut/dye it? Is Bill an only child or does his sister/brother hate him and why? Was Jack homeless as a teen because his parents kicked him out for constantly violating home rules and how does that affect his current parenting strategies?

Spend some time creating characters using the Character Study Guide on the next page. Just for fun, fill it out for a Disney Princess first.

MASTERING THE CRAFT OF WRITING

Exercise: Character Study Guide

Name: Age: Birthday/Sign:

Physical Characteristics

Draw a picture of your character.   List the physical characters next to the picture. Include hair, eyes, weight, scars, body type, shape of nose or ears, tattoos, ticks, etc.

Favorite Things: Pets:

Hobbies:

Dislikes:

Obsession:

Personal Triggers:

Transportation:

Education:

Shops: Shoes:

Family history:

Brothers/sisters:

Relationships: Birth order:

Parents:

Backstory:

What's in his/her pocket/purse/trunk/backpack?

Character Development Questions

- Are the characters compelling, sympathetic, or someone you can root for?
- Do the characters feel real and three-dimensional, with distinct voices, flaws, and virtues?
- Are their goals clear and proactive enough to influence the plot (not passive)?
- Do their motivations seem believable, with well-drawn and appropriate emotion?
- Are the secondary characters well-rounded and enhance the story rather than overwhelming the story or seeming like they should be cut?
- Are the relationships between the characters believable and not contrived?

The Main Character (MC)

(otherwise known as The Protagonist)

In American films, the audience expects the main character to be the first person to make a major decision. That's a good rule of thumb for books as well. It's not always true, but if it isn't, ask yourself how the reader will know who the MC (main character) is.

She is the one who will go on a journey with the reader, encounter devastating conflicts, and will end the journey a changed person (usually- there are exceptions, but my question remains… why? Why did you do it differently? If your reason is good, your story will be good also. It's not a matter of following the rule for the sake of rule following, but because it helps your reader stay in the story with you).

The Main character is the Somebody who in the following story structure formula:

Somebody (main character/protagonist) wants something (goal) but this happens (Inciting incident) and then this, this, this, and this (plot steps driven by conflict) happen until the final climax and resolution.

So… who is this Character? Why do they exist? What makes them unique and memorable? Are they likable (they don't have to be likable, but they must have something special that keeps the reader rooting for them)?

Why do they do the things they do? What makes them change? How do they react to stress, anxiety, manipulation, failure, or loss? Everyone reacts differently to that list dependent on their own history. What talents do they have that they don't know about?

Motivation is the next question. People don't do things in a vacuum. Something drives them to make decisions- good or bad. What is it? When did it happen? Why is it still affecting them? How does it change over the journey?

Personality: A developed character will have her own style, voice, reactions, and choices that are founded on the decisions you make as the writer. if you find it difficult to visualize your MC speaking to you, tools like the Myers-Briggs personality inventory (groups people into sixteen distinctive personality types and is based on Carl Jung's theory).

MASTERING THE CRAFT OF WRITING

Exercise: Think About It

What MC's do you remember years later?

Why do you remember them?

How did their past failures change them?

What was their reaction to having to change or did they change?

Scrooge? Gandalf? Sherlock Holmes?

Exercise: Create YOUR MC

What's memorable about your MC?

How does he/she react to difficulties?

What motivates your Main Character?

The Antagonist

You have your Main Character created, so what's next? His foil- the person(s), institution, or concept that opposes your MC's goal. As you can see from the list, it doesn't have to be a single person (although as a beginner writer, it's easier if your antagonist has a face).

But... the Antagonist is the HERO of his story. That means that he has his own motivations, goals, trials, journeys, failures, and backstory if you want him to be a full three-dimensional character that feels real.

One way to accomplish this is to create a character study for your Antagonist. I suggest doing one for every major player in your story.

What if they are an institution? These are common in today's storylines to the point where they are almost a cliché. It's the rich Wall Street guys, the evil bankers, the Church. Either way, you need to understand their motivation, history, and what's at stake if they fail. Give them a face for the reader to hate. For example, Mr. Potter in *It's a Wonderful Life* represents All Greedy Rich People. But what if Mr. Potter grew up poor, scrounging for food, and had a loved one die from starvation? Now his motivation is clearer. You can't visit that backstory in film, but there is room in a novel to investigate it.

Concepts are more difficult. Think of Galileo. Not only was he at opposition with the Church (institution), he was opposing current scientific belief (concept). If your Hero takes on current scientific beliefs, make sure you've done your research so that your character doesn't feel ignorant to the reader.

Motivation isn't an easy thing to understand for the Antagonist. A classic example is Iago's hatred of Othello. Literary experts have been trying to explain why he hated Othello enough to destroy him. I suspect that Shakespeare didn't care why. He needed someone slimy to move the story forward from a love story to a tragedy, and Iago, the sneaky lying snake in the grass, was the perfect foil for Othello. He's a character that's easy to hate, and yet, you want to see how all his machinations will destroy Othello.

Without a well-developed Antagonist to help move your character through the conflict, you will find the journey is short for your MC.

Some writers love their antagonist more than their protagonist. I'm not sure that's a bad thing!

Mastering the Craft of Writing

Exercise: Think About It

Your Favorite Bad Characters

What do you like about them?

What makes them memorable?

How are they the hero of their own story?

If your Antagonist is an institution, how are you going to present them so the reader sees them as the Antagonist?

If your Antagonist is a concept, what research will you need to do?

What motivates your Antagonist?

What specific conflicts are you building into your Antagonist?

The Sidekick

Why does Batman have Robin (and Alfred)? Because your MC doesn't exist in a vacuum. They are in a world populated with a variety of people. They have family members, friends, frenemies, real enemies, and these people keep your world grounded. These people are critical to world building and in showing your MC in a variety of situations.

Some of these characters have a specific role- being the MC's sidekick, or a close companion who is usually subservient to the MC (think Pancho to Don Quixote or Sam and Frodo in *Lord of the Rings*). They go on the journey with your MC.

Even antagonists can have sidekicks, though we tend to call them lackeys or henchmen.

Sidekicks have a critical role: they get your MC out of their head and give them someone to talk to so that they can explain choices and issues. Your MC will spend enough time alone, thinking, but for variety, you need the sidekicks in their life. These are the people who know the MC intimately enough to let them know when they're making a mistake or thinking the wrong way (not that they'll listen to that advice- at least mine never do!). Using dialogue to explain actions or tell bits of backstory.

Your Sidekicks have their own lives and opinions as well. They will offer their own point of view of any situation without being asked. They don't necessarily praise the MC or approve of her actions at the time, but they will have his back if needed.

Your Sidekick will have a way of seeing your MC as a flawed human who is still valuable even when they fail. They'll be there to help pick up the pieces afterwards, and sometimes, they'll ride into battle with the MC, knowing it'll be bad in the end.

Most importantly, they increase the conflict and raise the stakes. They get captured and tortured by bad guys. They get stuck in the middle and need to be rescued. They make bad choices that requires your MC to make decisions. They push the MC in a specific direction.

How many sidekicks can be in your novel? That depends on your story. Is it a story about a band of brothers/sisters out to conquer the world? How many of those characters are completely on the side of your MC? How many does your MC win over-- if any?

Populate your world with interesting flawed people.

Exercise: **Think About It**

Your Favorite Sidekicks

Who Are They?

What do you like about them?

How can an animal or an object be a sidekick?

Who does your MC need with him/her on their journey?

What does that character bring to the journey?

FIVE MINUTES TO SUCCESS

What's missing from your story that a specific sidekick can add to it effectively?

How does your sidekick increase the conflict and raise the stakes for your MC?

What does your sidekick do to help the MC grow and change?

Internal Flaw

You know what's boring?

An MC who is perfect and never makes a mistake or changes in any way.

Your MC needs to be flawed internally. Figuring out what that flaw is will develop a natural flow of conflict in your story. This flaw keeps your MC from achieving her final goal until she conquers it and moves past it. Others will use that flaw against her. They think they'll be able to predict her moves based on her past reactions.

For example, your MC is afraid of trying new things. She lives a simple orderly life and she likes it that way. She grew up in chaos and has spent her life trying to avoid conflict. What's the first thing you do as a writer? You start her journey by upsetting his orderly life. Every time she slips back into his comfort zone, you take it away. You know that given a choice between going home and continuing the journey, she'll chose going home. But there is no story if she stays home with her favorite wine and book. She has to try new things.

There are a variety of flaws.

For example, your MC:

puts work first,

puts money before people,

Five Minutes to Success

has low self-esteem and feels worthless,

has no dreams or vision,

doesn't think for herself,

refuses to grow up or make adult decisions,

relies on others for support,

is blinded by grief, greed, anger, etc.,

acts recklessly,

stays stuck in the past.

These are a few examples. I'm sure you'll be able to add to the list.

Exercise: Think about…

What internal flaws can you add to the list?

Pick one internal flaw and write about how having that internal flaw affects your MC

What new conflicts arise from adding an internal flaw to your characters?

Do only MC's have internal flaws?

Emotional Stakes

You know that your novel needs tension, but how? Part of the solution is including emotional stakes when you're plotting your MC's conflict steps. Increasing the emotional risks will drag your reader into the plot. They want to care about what your MC is feeling. Start with asking a few questions:

What does your MC want?

How does your MC feel and react when she doesn't get what she wants?

What does your MC need?

How does getting this change your MC?

What your MC wants starts out as his goal that he needs to accomplish but that you as a writer are going to keep him from reaching without a lot of pain. This goal usually is developed early from the inciting incident that jumpstarts the journey. Not getting what he wants should trigger an emotional reaction. That reaction can change as he grows and learns.

What he wants isn't necessarily what he needs. There is a serious difference between the two if you are writing a character-driven story and you want her to change by the end of the story. If he's unlikable at the beginning, the reader needs to know that if he's unlikable, at least he has a reason for his behavior.

Even if your MC isn't likable, readers want to go on his journey with him. They need a reason to do that. Are they curious? Do they know someone like him? Do they feel his behavior is justified?

When faced with a decision, will he go with his gut or will he change directions? As the writer, you're going to go with the one that gives you increased conflict. It's tempting to give him what he wants, but the story ends at that point.

So how do emotions affect conflict? What happens when you make a decision when you're angry, sad, or happy? Chances are it isn't the decision you'd make when you're in an emotionally level state.

Five Minutes to Success

Exercise: Journal (if You're Brave Enough)

Write about a time when you made a decision based on emotion and not logic.

The Backstory

The backstory is the history of your main character up to the point in time when your story begins. It is the experiences, failures, successes, relationships, and beliefs that affect how your MC (and other characters) respond to current challenges.

For example, your MC grew up dirt poor in the country and now she's rich-- but she is on the verge of losing everything because...

Why is she losing everything? Is she shady? Does she take short cuts? Is she naive or jaded? Where do the answers to these questions come from? Her personal backstory. This is more than "she grew up with a single mother who hated dirt and poverty but loved men".

An effective backstory explains why she makes the choices she does when she's in a jam or is facing conflict. Using it to explore her inner flaw and how it developed makes a deep character who feels real.

How much of it do you put in your book? Only the bits you need when you need it. Don't tell your reader anything he needs to know until he needs to know it. Writers like to think that the backstory drives the story, but while you need to know it, it's not the driving force.

If you've invested in creating a document with the complete backstory written out, you have two great choices. First, you can write Prequels based on events for your fans to read on your website. Or you can post the complete backstory for your website.

Where it doesn't belong is at the beginning of your story. It's a distraction and interferes with getting your reader hooked on your tale.

Backstory appears in Prequels as well.

"But I'm world building and the reader needs to know the rules." Nope. The reader needs to know the rule when your MC is breaking it. Weaving in the backstory makes the tale rich and provocative. Backstory is not your main story so don't let it overwhelm the story you're writing.

Backstory: Character Arc

Your story doesn't happen in a vacuum. There is a history behind it and a future ahead. As the writer, only you know the history and future for your characters. This knowledge is the backstory. It includes her family history, major and minor experiences, failures and successes, her school and work experiences, good and bad relationships, and even her bad haircut or clothing decisions. The backstory makes your characters come alive and breathe in the space you create for them.

Pieces of it will be revealed in your story as it develops and as you need them. Most of it will stay in your notes and in your brain. The temptation is to include all of it upfront in the prologue or first chapter, especially if you're building a complex world. Resist! Don't do a brain dump but use it as a rare spice delicately seasoning your writing. All of your characters have a backstory. Imagine including all that in your story! It'd lose its direction and impact!

How do you know what to include and what to leave out? Only include that which moves your story to the next plot step. What's critical? Ask yourself these questions:

Does it raise the stakes?

Does the Main Character feel squeezed by an event in his past that makes his current predicament worse? Was your MC passed over from a promotion at his last job and is hesitant to try again? What if his new boss is a woman who got the job instead of him?

Which events in your MC's past raise the stakes in your current story?

Does it explain fears?

I have a serious fear of bugs after a person showing us some in an aquarium tripped and dumped them on me. When do you need this bit of backstory? When I encounter a strange insect in my bed, not before.

What fears does your Main Character have and why does she have them?

Does it increase the intensity of the obstacles your Main Character encounters?

If your Main Character has avoided conflict all her life because her mother was a drama queen, what happens when she's faced with drama she can't avoid?

What part of the backstory makes the conflict your MC faces more difficult?

What failures has she experienced before the story began?

Does it explain her motivations?

Mastering the Craft of Writing

If your Main Character runs towards danger instead of away, what motivates him to do that? Is he the oldest child assigned the responsibility of keeping his siblings safe, only to fail at it?

Exercise: Backstory notes

Family history:

# of siblings

Place in family

Relationship with family members

School/Work experience:

Good ones:

Bad ones:

What was the take away from his/her school/work experiences?

Fears:

Where do these come from? What experiences fed them?

Motivations:

What past experiences drive your Main Character's motivations? Why?

Conflict:

How does your MC react to conflict? What happened in the past to cause her to react that way?

Five Minutes to Success

Tics, Mutterings, and Other Odd Mannerisms

Field Trip Time!

It's time to go people watching, writer! My favorite place is the food court at the mall. All ages and groupings show up while I'm there. I target a different writing skill each time I go. Sometimes it's to listen to dialogue and guess the story behind it. This time it's to look at how people move, act, respond to various interactions, and learn what makes them individual and unique.

Your characters should have that same feeling about them. When you are defining your character, visualize them walking and sitting down. Do they pull up the legs of their pants before sitting like the old men in church on Sunday morning? Are they nervous and tap on the table or kick the chair leg? Do they walk around something three times before claiming it like a dog getting to nap on the kitchen floor?

It's very easy to fall into clichés when creating characters who have mannerisms. You can avoid it by making the mannerisms character-driven. Ask yourself why a character does that. Think about yourself. What unique and distinctive mannerisms and habits do you have? I always have a pen in my pocket. And it's not any old pen, but one kind that I buy in packs of six. When I'm stressed, I have an Arizona tea lid that I push in and out until the clicking drives people insane. I have the pen because as a writer, I'm taking notes constantly in the notebook stashed in my purse or in my car, and I'm very picky about pens. The ink needs to flow exactly correctly or the whole process annoys me and I can't write. The tea lid habit came when I taught school and some of the students pushed my last nerve. I'd click it several times before I responded. Your character may not know why he does things, but his creator should.

You have to be careful that you don't rely on these character traits when you're writing. Save them for appropriate reactions to a situation.

Five Minutes to Success

Exercise: Field Trip

Ready for the field trip? Go to a place populated by people (a fast food restaurant after school, the mall food court, the park on a sunny day). Take notes!

What do people do with their hands and feet while they're talking?

How do people decide which table to select and how do they claim it?

How do people of various ages respond to a situation? (Ordering food, getting out their money, drinking)

What do people do when they are in a large group? How is it different when they are alone?

Use as many words as possible to describe people walking by you:

Which emotions cross people's faces? Why do they have that emotion?

Make a list of mannerisms:

When did you see those mannerisms? What were they doing?

How does dress/shoes affect mannerisms? Or does it?

Which habits were disgusting?

What did they do to express love or caring?

Summary:

What did you learn about people while on this field trip?

Which tics, mutterings, or mannerisms fit your characters and why? Are they unique and distinctive or cliché and overused?

Keeping A Story Bible

Eight years after I finished a book, a cover illustrator texted me, "What color are her eyes?" Did I know? I've written six books since that one. Was I going to have to scan the book for that tiny detail? That's why you need a Story Bible!

You have all these details floating in your brain about your work in progress, and in the beginning it's easy to keep them straight. As you get deeper into the writing and editing process, they become all muddled into a big Katamari bubble (A Japanese video game where you roll around collecting things as your blob gets larger and larger until it's large enough to pick up an elephant or a building).

The answer is the Story Bible- an organized reference guide/journal that tracks facts.

Authors use a variety of methods to accomplish this task. The trick is to find the one that works for you and work it. None of these will work if you don't keep up with it. It can be kept online, with Scrivener, in Word, in a notebook, on storyboards. I use large Post-It sheets that ring my writing area for easy access. When I complete the book, I roll them up, write the title and date on the outside and stash them in a wrapping paper organizer.

The level of organization depends your own needs. Some people use large notebooks and tag every section. Others throw it all in a notebook and leaf through it to find the specific content needed. There is no wrong way. It can be complex or simple. You can color-code it, write it in pencil, ink, or crayon, or write sidewise so you can find it faster.

What goes in it?

- The BIG concept
- The ten-word log line
- Character studies
- Family trees
- Settings and details about specific settings
- Conflict ideas
- Plot steps
- Legends
- Research
- World details
- Society Rules
- Timeline
- Religion
- Anything else relating to the story such as reference photos, maps, tide charts, calendar, holidays, trash pickup day, vehicles, stores, etc. The list is endless.

Mastering the Craft of Writing

Exercise:

Visualize your story bible. Draw it below. Now-- go create it!

Story Development

What Is it?

When you're writing a story, you're moving characters from the beginning through the middle to the end. Story development is the process of making sure your characters are moving, growing, and even dancing if the story calls for it.

So what is it?

A novel is full of scenes that tell a story. Those scenes are connected by the characters interacting with each other, with conflict, and with themselves. In order for it to work, every scene has a role to play. Some explore internal conflict while others may be all action.

No, really, what is it?

Story development is the process of looking at the plot steps to make sure that there is a cause and an effect that builds to the next choice. The action and decision that a character makes on page ten changes the story and propels it to the next big conflict which has its own cause and effect that drives the character(s) to the next major plot step.

When the feedback about your work in progress is "eh, not much happened," you know you are either imitating a bad French film or that your conflict is weak. The solution is to look at each chapter and plot the conflict. Who has it? What does it push your character to choose next? Is it worse because of her actions and choices?

Someone causes something to happen which causes something worse to happen which causes something else even more horrific to happen as your character makes one bad decision after another.

The concepts of plot, tension, conflict, inciting incident, and twists and turns being done in a three Act model will be explored in-depth in this section. It will take the character development you did in the previous section and help you apply to plot so that you end up with a character-driven plot that contains emotional impact for the reader. Pull down the safety bar. The rollercoaster is heading towards the large, straight up rail. Bumps to follow shortly!

Five Minutes to Success

The Ten Word Pitch

Ask any writer what they're writing and your eyes glaze over as they talk non-stop about the new project. At the end of it, you aren't sure if you'd read it or not because your ears and head hurt. The truth is that most of us can't give a precise description of our work because it's 385 pages full of twists and turns. And yet, being able to express it simply is a marketing tool worth learning. I suggest developing it early in the development process and using it as writing map.

Start with Somebody:

> Who is your MC?
>
> The new 6th grader, Sunshine
>
> Thomas, a laid-off welder

Next: **Goals**: What does your MC want?

> Sunshine wants to fit in, or go home, or turn back time
>
> Thomas wants a job, or his wife back, or to find his lost dog

BUT: The but is a big deal. It's what is preventing your MC from achieving their goal. It's the inciting incident, the disturbance in their life that starts their journey.

> But: No matter what Sunshine does, she can't make friends, or her mother dies, or…

But: Thomas loses a hand in a freak accident, or his wife remarries, or he's ill, or…

And this, this, this, and maybe **this HAPPENS**… this is your major plot steps. There should be at least three (more on this in depth under plot)

UNTIL: Climax- the major climatic moment at the end

And… **Resolution.** (Wait, I don't want to give the story away! No seriously, I'm not telling the ending). Write it! The people you're pitching want to know the ending.

It ends up looking like this:

Someone

wants something

but this happens

and this, this, this, and definitely THIS TOO

until climax and resolution.

Five Minutes to Success

Exercise: *Your Turn*

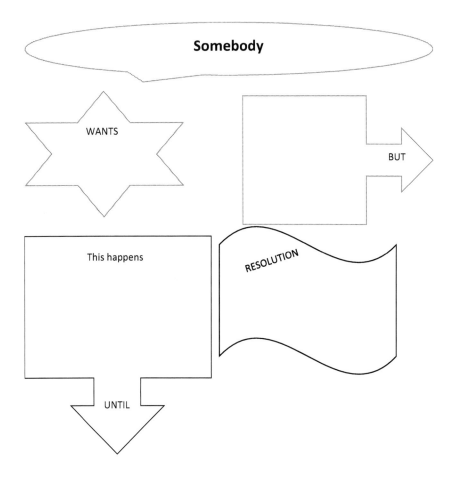

Write out your final thoughts:

Show, Don't Tell, and Specifics Sell

That's one of my favorite phrases because it's so true. Show, don't tell is an old one. Right now let's talk about specifics.

Here's an example sentence:

Brenda was embarrassed by her toddler's unruly behavior at the grocery store.

Grammatically correct, but not great. It's passive (was embarrassed by), it's telling (was embarrassed), and it's vague. You can't really picture the scene. Let's contrast it to this:

Brenda ducked behind the doughnut display, face burning as her toddler marched down the refrigerated meat counter, stomping on the steaks.

So much better.

It's active (she's doing something, not having something done to her), she's showing embarrassment (hiding, face burning) so I don't have to tell you she's embarrassed, and... vague? Nope. This is a scene you can picture.

Here are a few more boring sentences.

Susie was very happy that the day had turned out to be so nice.

Jack got angry with Bob, yelling at him for ten minutes.

The cat looked very comfortable.

Those are all grammatically correct, but how could you make each one stronger?

Exercise: Think About It

Look through your own work sentence by sentence. What is vague that could be made specific?

Theme

What is the heart of your story about? Not the details about character or plot, but the foundation of your story, the part out of sight? That's your theme. It's the unseen driving force that makes the reader sigh with emotional contentment when they finish or leaves them pondering the mysteries of the universe because you made those thoughts pop into their head. Oh, the power of theme! It can right wrongs, organize a movement, change an attitude, or simply make a good book a deeper read. It moves your story off the written page into the hearts and minds of your reader.

But what is it? Think of it as the big concept surrounding your story. It may be vague, a word, or a phrase. Grief! Loss! Overcoming! Survival! Recovery! Personal Strength! Love Heals! The List is endless.

Add to the list:

Why do you need a theme? Well, you don't. You can write a solid story about interesting characters with intriguing plot twists, like eating an off-brand chocolate bar. When your reader finishes, they set your book aside and move on to the next one. However, if you immerse your story in a theme, there is a richness and depth that is universal to many human experiences. It helps them identify and relate to the story in spite of the characters and settings. It taps into the common life experience and gives one more to balance out the world. It's what makes a reader reread a book and fall in love with it.

It adds two more important ingredients: it keeps your writing focused and it drives your conflict. When you are trying to figure out if a scene belongs or should be deleted, ask if it enriches and reinforces your theme, and if it does, keep it. If the conflict isn't serious enough, ask yourself how the theme would affect it.

Determine your theme early in the writing process. Mull it over in your mind. Research it and visualize it with feet—meaning, picture conflicts based on the theme.

Five Minutes to Success

Exercise: Make a list of the conflicts in your story.

```
┌─────────────────────────────────────┐
│                                     │
│                                     │
│                                     │
│                                     │
└─────────────────────────────────────┘
```

The next suggestion sounds a bit silly, but it works.

Forget about it. Let your sub consciousness mentally play with the theme for a while. It may start popping up in your dreams, and in your conversations. You'll see examples of it in news stories or in everyday life. People may tell you stories that are colored by your theme. I call this "The New Car Syndrome". You know how once you buy a new car, you see identical ones on the road all the time when you never noticed them before? That'll happen with your theme. You will be so immersed in your theme that it'll leak over to your writing.

How do you pick a theme?

Sometimes your Main character will dictate it. Sometimes the subject matter will. Mostly, it's driven by your personal passions and demons. Use them happily! But, a word of warning. If you let your theme overrun your story, it can end up preachy and have the opposite effect. Just like too much rich chocolate makes you ill, the same can be true of your theme.

Does Your Theme Drive Conflict?

Now that your basic theme is in your mind, time to brainstorm how it will drive your characters to grow and change while experiencing conflict.

Remember- conflict is a critical part of keep your story moving forward and if it's based on critical story telling techniques, it'll make your tale a rich read.

There are two ways to approach using your theme. The first is to tell the reader the theme repeatedly. (Nope, let's not do that!) I recently saw a Singaporean drama whose theme was The Same Justice for Everyone. How do I know that was the theme? The characters told me so a couple of times during each episode. I got it! Move on!

The more effective way is to soak the conflict in your theme. Think about your protagonist. How does she make a decision when faced with conflict? Does she believe in the theme or is skeptical about it? How does your antagonist use the theme to force your protagonist into a corner?

For example: Your theme is "Different isn't bad or good, it's just different". Let's brainstorm that a bit. Each decision you make should affect the story and your conflict is now theme driven. You won't use all these ideas (have plenty so you can reject some). Your protagonist may have a deep-seated fear of strangers that she has to face directly in order to achieve her goals. Your antagonist may use that fear to get what he wants from the protagonist. The Grandmother might reinforce the fear with her stories. What conflicts does this theme of difference help you develop?

Mastering the Craft of Writing

Exercise: Brainstorm Here

Your turn!

Theme:

What conflict does your theme cause each character? List them below.

Character #1	Character #2	Character #3	Character #4	Character #5

Scene Development

Just like a good movie has three (maybe four) acts, so should your novel. Think of every new chapter as a new scene. This scene has a beginning, a middle, and an end, as well as a problem. It also includes setting, emotion, and conflict.

So… what has to happen in each chapter?

You have some decisions to make:

What's the big conflict in this scene?

Whose POV (point of view) is it?

What has to happen to get to the next plot point?

Is the setting critical to the plot or character development?

After you know those critical things, the next step is to decide where to begin. My suggestion is NOT to begin at the beginning. Start closer to the middle. Try cutting the first page or so and see if the scene works without it. Chances are your story will be stronger if you do that. This is called Starting Late.

If you Start Late, you should plan on Ending Early. Give the reader only the information they need to know at this point. End with a twist, a surprise, a revelation, a new piece of information, a secret, goal failure (or success), character grows or reverts, increases tension, or a new decision is made.

How soon should you end the scene? Has the big conflict happened? Has the plot moved forward towards the next plot point? Did character growth happen?

But this is just a scene where she meets her new dog. Does it need all this work? Absolutely. If you have a scene where nothing happens, cut it! It's pure fluff that doesn't move your story where it needs to go next.

Five Minutes to Success

Exercise: Visualize/Illustrate

Pick a scene that's fighting you. Close your eyes and walk through it.

Use your senses.

What do you see, hear, feel, touch, smell? How's the weather?

What's the attitudes of the characters in the room? What are they doing to show their attitude?

Imagine the conflict. Listen to your characters speak. What are they saying? How does it end?

Play it like a movie in your mind. If you're missing something, go for a walk by yourself (or with the dog) and replay it.

Chew on it until it bursts to life in living color.

Answer the questions above here:

Narration: Who's Telling the Story?

Before you write a single word in a new story or novel, you must choose your narrator. With three major options (and a fourth for very special circumstances), think carefully about your decision. Once the novel is done, go back and consider the story as it evolved. Did you choose the right one? If not, can you change it?

In skilled hands, a novel can have more than one narrator (for example, in a story with two main characters, one could be the first-person narrator and the other could be seen in third person limited), but this can get tricky. If this is your first novel, you might be better off choosing one and sticking with it.

First Person

First person is "I." As in, "I opened the door." The narrator in a first person scene is the main character in the scene, like a movie camera seeing directly through her eyes. The reader can only see what she sees, hear what she hears, feel what she feels, etc. So if I'm writing a first person scene and "I" am sitting in a classroom, "I" can't know what's going on in the hall. If it's important for the reader to know this, we must either find a way for the main character/first person narrator to find out later (as in, someone tells "me" about it), or the door has to open so "I" can hear or see what's going on.

The advantage of first person is that it's the closest possible narrator to the story. The reader feels like they're really there, because she's following along with the person everything is happening to. It's a great way to pull a reader in fast. The disadvantage is that the reader is limited to one character's point of view. This can be helpful in something like a mystery, when we don't want the reader to know more than the main character, but sometimes detrimental in something like a thriller, when we might want the reader to have outside knowledge of some threat that increases the conflict.

Third Person Limited

This is the most common narrator in fiction. We are seeing the action from outside one main character, like a movie camera focused on one person in a scene. So: John opened the door. John is our main character, and this scene is in his point of view (more on point of view later). We can hear his thoughts (example: John opened the door. *Sure hope nobody's home*, he thought.), which are usually shown in italics. (Side note: once you establish this, it's not necessary to say "he thought" anymore. Just type the words in italics and we know it's a thought. This works for all limited narrators.) It's third person limited because we are focusing on John in this scene. We can't know what Mary is thinking even if she's in the same room. We see what John sees, we hear what he hears. It's a recipe for head-hopping, which is a Bad Thing we'll discuss in a later chapter.

The advantage of third person limited is that it puts us into a point of view character's head and remains focused on their part of the story, which helps readers feel grounded and attached to that character. The disadvantage is that just like first person, if John is inside the classroom, he can't know what's going on in the hall. And the Bad Thing of head-hopping most often pops up in third person limited.

Third Person Omniscient

Many writers believe this is the hardest narrator to write successfully. It's not in vogue at the moment of this writing, but all things cycle through, and it surely will be popular again soon, so it's worth considering. The "third person" part of this narrator is the same as the third person limited. It's not an "I" story, it's a "He" story. John opened the door. The difference is the omniscient part. An omniscient narrator is almost a character of their own. It's the top-down camera view, the eyes of Someone watching the story unfold, or telling the story to someone else. A story that begins, "A long time ago in a country very like our own..." would be omniscient. There's someone telling this story. They have their own thoughts about the action and might share them with the reader, as in, "Little did John know that what was behind the door would change the rest of his life." John can't know that. The only way a reader can be told it is if there's a godlike storyteller weaving the tale.

The benefit of omniscient narrator is that the narrator sees all. He can see John in the classroom. He can also see Suzy in the hallway, and Joe on another continent. He can hear all of their thoughts and know all their motivations. The disadvantage is basically the same. It's harder for a reader to connect with one character when she's seeing them all. It's very easy to get dizzy jumping from one character to another; this is why only the most skilled writers can pull this off well. The other disadvantage is that it's currently viewed as old fashioned, except in books aimed at young children.

Second Person

The second person is you. Writing in second person is common in text-based computer games and "Choose Your Adventure" type books. Example: You walk down the musty hallway, smelling mold and decay. The darkness plays tricks on your vision. Most novels are not written in second person, but in specific circumstances it can be necessary.

The advantage is that it puts the reader smack-dab in the middle of the action. It's no longer "me" or "John" that the bad stuff is happening to. It's you. The disadvantage is that it gets boring fast, and is prone to filtering, a Bad Thing we'll talk about in the editing section.

Mastering the Craft of Writing

Exercise: Practice

Change the following sentences into third person:

    I peered out the window into the purple twilight.

    The hammer smashed down onto my finger. Gosh, that's painful.

Change the following sentences into first person:

    John picked up the puppy, inhaling the sweet scent of clean fur.

    The puppy licked John's face.

Choosing a narrator

So how do you choose?

Sometimes the choice of narrator is organic. You just feel the story from one particular point of view and go with it. But usually it's a decision process, and here's how I approach it.

The first thing I consider is if I can tell the story entirely from one character's point of view. If I choose to tell this tale in first person (I peered out the window), then nothing "I" can't see can be told unless someone else tells "me" about it. When I'm making this decision, I'll try to think through my plot, figuring out how one main character could possibly witness or learn about every important plot point. If I can make it work, I might choose first person as my narrator for the intimate, personal feel. First person reads like a diary, and that helps a reader connect with the main character right up front.

The danger of first person is "I." It's very tempting to overuse it. I peered out the window. I saw leaves rustling in the trees. Turning away from the window, I walked over to the couch and sat down. I leafed through a fashion magazine. See how that's horrible? If you're writing in first person, you have to figure out ways to turn the story away from "I" and out toward the world. I peered out the window. Leaves rustled through the trees. Turning away, I walked over the couch and sat down. The magazine I'd been reading last night was still open in the counter.

One dumb fashion article after another. By cutting down the "I"s and changing some sentence structure, the second example reads a lot easier.

What if I can't figure out a way for one character to tell the whole story? Then I have a couple of choices: either third person limited (because omniscient just isn't an option for me personally. Maybe someday, but not anytime soon.), or mix-and-match.

You can have multiple point of view characters in third person limited. We can see the classroom scene from John's point of view, then we can jump out into the hallway and see what Mary's up to out there from her point of view. The catch is that you can only have one point of view character per scene. So if we are making that hallway hop, we need a chapter break or scene break so the reader can reorient into someone else's head. More on that in the point of view section.

Resist the temptation to have a bunch of point of view characters. The fewer, the better. If we're constantly jumping from one character's scenes to another, it's much harder for a reader to connect with each character and care about them. And if the reader doesn't care about the characters, they put the book down and walk away.

Mix-and-match can be effective if used properly. This is where you have (at least) two point of view characters, and one of them is your first-person narrator while the other(s) is/are told in third person. You might have a first-person scene, where John is your first person narrator: I looked out at the classroom, over the heads of my bored students. We'd see the classroom scene directly through John's eyes, with John himself telling the story. Scene break (a couple of spaces between paragraphs, or a new chapter). Mary clopped down the hall, new shoes echoing on the scuffed tiles. And we go on through this scene looking at what Mary is doing. She's not telling the scene herself, but we are watching her experience it. The reader will naturally feel closer to John (the "I" character), but will still be able to see Mary (and possibly others) doing things that John can't know about. This can be very useful for increasing tension, as in this example: I reached for the doorknob.

If we're strictly in first person, then we have no idea what's behind the door. But if we're playing mix-and-match, and in the last scene we saw Mary step into the hallway shadows with an ax, now we know very well what's behind the door waiting for our first-person narrator. The tension is a lot higher as "I reached for the doorknob."

Mastering the Craft of Writing

Exercise: Think About It

What scenes in your story can be told from a single point of view?

Which ones can't, and how will you handle these?

Plot Development

PLOT IS...

Rising tension

Rising suspense

Rising emotional intensity

Rising stakes

Bigger and bigger obstacles

Bigger and bigger confrontations

Bigger and bigger failures

Increasingly dramatic scenes

Plot is a twisty roller-coaster that finally ends, leaving you breathless and ready to read again!

(Draw your favorite roller-coaster here, just because... it's fun?)

Digging Deeper

I keep mentioning that four letter word, **PLOT**, but what is it? Simply put, plot is the series of actions that take your story from page 1 to THE END. They are the main events that help the characters face conflict.

Plot starts as soon as your character encounters conflict and has to make a choice. This choice may move them back or forward, but staying in one place is no longer a possibility.

If you think of it as… THIS HAPPENS and THEREFORE THAT… you can see how important plot is to create a story full of conflict.

For example, the cat dropped a mouse in her owner's coffee and therefore that…

You have a plot step leading towards the next major event.

When plotting a work, I think of it like this:

Inciting Incident

Plot Step 2- Rising Tension

Plot Step 3- Increasing Tension

Plot Step 4- Internal Conflict

All is Lost

Plot Step 6 The Rebuild

Climax

Resolution

You can have more plot steps, of course, but these are the critical ones. I do it on one page and post that page on the wall where I can see it when I start writing. The plot steps may change as I write and I allow that to happen since this is a basic "get from here to there" thing. I may exclude a step as well if it doesn't fit my work in progress.

Not everyone plots and that's ok. (see section on Pantser or Plotter) It may mean that during the editing process you'll have to spend time looking at tension and how it moves as well as for holes in the story (plot holes) that keep it from making sense to the reader. There is no one way to write, but the requirements for a good story remain the same either way.

You'll notice I don't start with the typical expositional, currently known as "info dump," at the beginning. The practice of a slow opening that defines character, setting, and world view is out of fashion. It slows down your story and tells your reader more than they need to know. It's more effective to show your main characters in action making decisions based on their goals and motivations. Never tell your readers what they need to know until they need to know it.

Mastering the Craft of Writing

Try plotting your work:

Inciting Incident:

Plot Step 2- Rising Tension:

Plot Step 3- Increasing Tension:

Plot Step 4- Internal Conflict: All is Lost:

Plot Step 6 The Rebuild:

Climax:

FIVE MINUTES TO SUCCESS

Resolution:

Exercise: Process This

What worked with this process?

How awkward did it feel?

What didn't work?

What would you change to make it work for you?

Tension

Is it Rising or Falling? What is it? A soufflé?

Rising Tension

Picture a rubber band. Pull it tight. Tighter. Are you wincing because you know if it breaks that the snap will hurt? That's tension. Actually, it's rising tension. Take that rubber band and put it on a wooden rubber band gun now. Add another ten or twenty rubber bands. Aim it at your sister. And the gun breaks, blasting all the rubber bands at her… the tension is rising high now. The stakes have increased drastically.

In your novel, rising tension refers to the conflicts, character flaws, twists and turns that lead to the climax. One event, emotion, feeling, failure after another leads the reader up to the precipice, like a sheep to slaughter. They stay up all night reading, turning the pages as rapidly as possible as you torture their brain. That's a sign of good rising tension!

With each plot step, the stakes need to increase and put more pressure on your protagonist. Failure becomes costlier. That fatal character flaw puts your main character deeper in the quagmire. Don't rescue your character. Put her in the worst possible situation and make it even worse. This is where you have to be a brutal writer.

But it's hard to figure out where your tension isn't strong without help. A critical thing to ask a beta reader is when they lost interest. That will tell you where your tension lags and needs a boost. The resolution to this is character driven conflict. More CONFLICT!

Falling Tension

You know how after the party ends and everyone leaves and all that's left is cleaning up the mess? That's Falling Tension (known as falling action by some). After the climax, it's the rest of the story- tying up the loose ends, resolving all the left-over bits and pieces, and mopping up after messy characters.

Exercise: Visualize

Draw a picture of your current plot steps. Pretend it's a rollercoaster.

Where does it rise and fall?

MASTERING THE CRAFT OF WRITING

Conflict

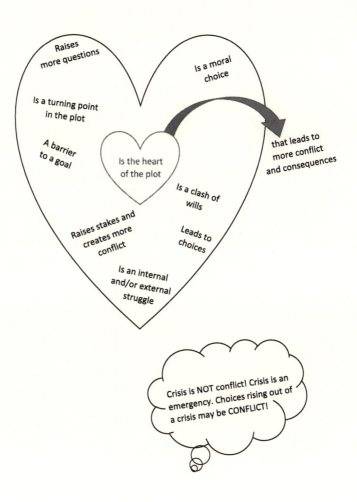

What Is CONFLICT and Why is it IMPORTANT?

Conflict is a barrier blocking the character's goal.

It creates drama

Plants a question in the reader's mind

> Will she escape?

> Will she be eaten alive by the dinosaurs?

The Question raise the stakes and creates more conflict at the end of scene which can be either a set-back, turnback, or a reversal of fortune.

It's the Turning Point in the plot.

Escalate the conflict

Your character:

Wants something badly-- desire denied creates internal conflict

Can't achieve their goal-- how does your character respond to roadblocks and adversity?

Tries to resolve the conflict by taking meaningful action

Good Conflict requires

Good opposition (even if it's only internal)

The antagonist counters the protagonist's attempts to solve the problem with force and cunning. (Not invincible or weak- but an annoyance out to ruin well-laid plans. Remember-- The

ANTAGONIST is the hero of their own story with their own flaws, agenda, and story!)

Opposition + Challenge + Obstacles to goal= plot!

Exercise: Reflect/journal:

What resonates with you from this section?

Inciting Incident

One of the hardest things for a new writer is figuring out where their story begins. If you start with the inciting incident within the first ten pages not only will you avoid the dreaded info dump, but you'll capture your audience's attention immediately.

The inciting incident is THE EVENT that triggers your protagonist to move out of their comfort zone to accomplish a goal. It's the big thing that disrupts their current normal that makes it impossible for them to stay where they are, content and happy.

Imagine this, your protagonist is watching Jeopardy and answering all the questions. All she wants is to finish her show in peace.

But… as the writer, your goal is to disrupt her and get her off the couch into action.

That disruption is your inciting incident. It starts your hero/antihero on a journey of change and insight and takes your readers along for the ride.

List as many as you think of in one minute:

Five Minutes to Success

Exercise: Think again

Now, take a minute and answer these questions: What does your protagonist want?

What's her goal?

How does her character determine how she approaches accomplishing this goal?

What Inciting Incidents will get your protagonist off the couch?

Where Does Your Story Begin?

If you're like most first-time authors, your story starts in the wrong place. First-timers always want to set the scene and reveal the backstory behind their characters' lives so the reader is grounded before the action begins. But that's the right word, grounded. As in, your story is going to grind to a halt if you do this.

Don't be sad. I did it too. My first published novel opens with a tense scene where our main character faces a wall of magic flames. She has to walk through the fire in a ceremony to see if she will be gifted with magic powers (here's a surprise...she gets them). The day she receives her gift for magic is the inciting action for the story, because everything else that happens is because of that event. But when I wrote the first draft, I started with breakfast. Breakfast that morning, chores... milking freakin' cows, for Pete's sake. I thought it was important to establish her boring, pastoral life before she was swept up in a new world of power and danger. It wasn't. Her boring, pastoral life was boring. So I cut the porridge, cut the cows, and got straight into the thing that set the rest of the book in motion.

What's your inciting incident?

The inciting incident is the thing that makes the rest of the book happen. It's Harry Potter getting a letter from Hogwarts. It's Gandalf telling Frodo that the pretty gold ring has to go. It's the rabbits leaving their home in search of somewhere to live that's not about to be plowed under for a housing development. And it's where your story should begin.

The rule of good writing is to never tell the reader anything they don't need to know until the moment they need to know it. Can you imagine if *Star Wars* started with a history of the Galactic Senate, a Skywalker family tree, a discussion of the nature of the Force, and a genealogy of Alderaan's royal family? Of course you can't. Those things are important, and we will eventually need to know them, but NOT RIGHT NOW. Right now we need to jump into the action, and the inciting incident is the droids with the secret plans escaping the Imperial attack and landing on Tatooine. So that's where the movie starts.

One of the most common things I hear in writing groups is, "Well, you just have to stick with it until Chapter Ten. That's when it really gets good." Awesome...why are Chapters One through Nine in there? I want to start reading your story when it "gets good." If the information in Chapters One through Nine are important to understand the characters and world and motivations, weave them in as we go. I don't have to know that the Force is a thing until Luke needs to learn how to use it. I don't have to know the Empire has built a Death Star until we come out of hyperspeed on top of it. So don't tell me. Get me into the action and drizzle in the backstory as you go.

As a general rule, if something happened before the inciting event of your story, it's backstory and does not belong in Chapter One. Family history? World building in fantasy or sci-fi? Magic systems or alien biology? History of Leonardo DaVinci? Not now. Tell me when I need to know them. For now, it's enough to know that we're on a non-Earth planet and the aliens can fly and read minds. I don't need to know how they developed wings, or how their government is set up. I just need to know who the hero is, and what's happened to change things in his life so that now he has to do something. Something worth writing a book about.

Consider your manuscript. Where does your story really start (not your book, your story). If you had to sum up your story in a few sentences, what would you say? Remember the important parts: Character, Conflict, and Stakes. Who is he? What does he want? Why can't he have it? What happens if he doesn't get it? Thinking about those key points will help you determine how to rearrange your story so it starts as late as possible in the action, at the moment the quest really begins.

Five Minutes to Success

Exercise: Think about it

Where does your current story begin?

Is it with your inciting incident?

What is your inciting incident? Is it big enough?

What can you cut from your story's opening and weave in later when we need to know it?

Figure 2: Plot Structure Chart #1

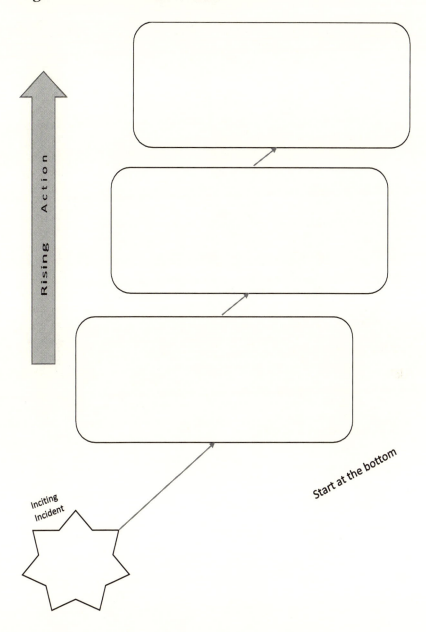

External Conflict

A good story has multiple, varied, layered levels of conflict that build suspense. It has turns and reversals with rising tension and forces change.

External conflict is the tool that helps you achieve that. It helps you increase suspense and emotional intensity.

A few external conflicts are:

    Character vs Character

    Character vs Nature/Environment

    Character vs Society

    Character vs Values/Beliefs

    Character vs Organization

    Character vs Laws/Politics

    Character vs History

    Character vs Supernatural

Exercise:

Highlight the ones in your current work.

Star one or two you'd like to explore more.

Go BIG BIGGER BIGGER!

Add more...

Obstacles

Confrontations

Failures

What is your work missing? How can you increase the conflict?

Internal Conflict = Character Growth

Internal conflict is:

In the mind

The dilemma inside the character and its impact on the character's decisions

Based on universal emotions-- inner needs, desires, beliefs, turmoil

It strikes at a vulnerability that they MUST confront

Psychological

The character bonds not just with people but with places, objects, memories. Show us the pull of the connection. What holds your character so tightly that they can't let it go?

When plotting this, it can go anywhere in plot line. I tend to put it near the end where my characters have to win battles within themselves before they can move forward. They've failed and retreat inside themselves until they find the strength to face their personal dragons and defeat them at whatever cost.

This is where you see character growth and change.

It happens when their character flaw holds them back and keeps them from achieving their goals, and I build it in from the beginning.

Mastering the Craft of Writing

Exercise: Think About:

What is your character's fatal flaw?

How has it kept him from accomplishing her goals?

What kinds of conflict and failure will make him examine himself and force him to change his course?

What does she do battle with internally?

Five Minutes to Success

Twists, Surprises, Red Herrings, and Reversals

You have your plot steps neatly in place. You are moving your protagonist towards the final trial and everything is going smoothly- except...

It's too predictable. What's a writer to do?

When this happens to me, I go to the mall food court, get a large Diet Coke, and people watch. The question I ask about the people I see is, "What surprising thing is this person hiding? What's their secret?"

A good plot twist has a foreshadowing detail earlier in the story. It may be a small detail or hint for the reader to file away. If you include a red herring or two, your reader will be kept guessing and your details won't be a plot spoiler. (Red herring= a detail that is a bit of misdirection that leads the reader towards an incorrect assumption.)

A reversal is a radical change in the direction of the plot. The "bad guy is the good guy and good guy is the bad guy" kind of thing.

There are a couple of famous (infamous) strategies you should know.

Deus ex machine: Don't use this one! It's cheating! This means that something or someone magically appears with all the answers and saves the day. There are no hints or details in the story that set it up.

Unreliable Narrator: This is when the narrator reveals at the end that the narrator hasn't told you the truth and that everything you've read is garbage. The real story is something completely different. There are times when this trick works well, but make sure that there's something in your story that the reader can identify as the basis for this change or it'll feel like manipulation.

Flashback: Often used to provide background information that the author can't figure out how to include any other way, it lets the character recall information and facts previously hidden from the reader. It may make the reader view the character differently or explain a behavior that didn't make sense earlier. This is a common strategy. Use at your own risk.

There are more. Google them under "plot twists" if you're curious.

Five Minutes to Success

Exercise: Wonder About

What twists and surprises are in your work? Do they work?

Are there clues hidden in the text so that a savvy reader can spot them?

What have you read/watched that had plot twists that surprised you?

All Is Lost - The Darkest Day

Everything's going wrong for your protagonist and it's all their own fault. They've failed, screwed up, isolated themselves from help, and are at the lowest point of their lives. They're ready to give up and go home, back where it's safe and they can hide under a blanket in their bed for the rest of their lives. That's the All Is Lost Plot Point.

Nobody likes him. Everyone hates him… he's at the worm - eating part of his life. That or become worm food. Those seem to be his only choices. You've driven him to this point and he wallows in his pain, fear, and anger. The emotions run deep at this plot point. He may cry from frustration or break things in his anger.

Good job, writer! You've set him to go through the pain of change. You've taken him from seed to sprout and now he must push hard to pull away the dirt and emerge as a plant soaking in the sunshine.

It's a bit tricky to not be manipulative here but to actually tap authentic, real feelings. The more authentic you are, the more the reader will be there with your character, feeling his emotions.

Exercise: Journal or visualize

Tap into the feelings

What was your personal darkest moment in life?

How did you feel?

What snapped you out of it?

What can you borrow from that experience to write about authentic pain and emotion?

Climax

You grabbed your water bottle and some granola bars. You put on sweat-absorbing socks and well broke-in hiking shoes. You tell someone where you're going and check the weather one more time. You have a hat for the sun, bug spray, and sunscreen. You've been hiking smaller hills and now you tackle the big one. A couple of hours later, you approach the top. You made it. The view of the world below your feet is breathtaking.

That's the climax of your story- the thing everything in your work has been building for. All that plot, character development, settings, tension, and conflict builds for this moment and BOOM! Everything explodes into a scary awesomeness full of emotion and personal satisfaction.

The struggle is over. Goals are attained (or not). Characters have grown (or not). The reader wants to feel something at this point-- happy, sad, satisfied, justified, angry, etc. This is the time to let your feelings fly and watch them land with a satisfying impact.

Your instinct may be to hold back at this point. There is a fine line between over the top and just right. It will take a couple of edits to reach the right temperature.

Five Minutes to Success

Exercise: Visualize/Illustrate

Close your eyes and dream a little. What does the final conflict look like? Who's there? Where is it? What are the feelings attached to the scene? Did your protagonist achieve their goal? If not, what did they achieve?

Once you have the scene in your head, draw it below. Add as many details as you can recall and add new ones.

Figure 3: Plot Structure Chart #2

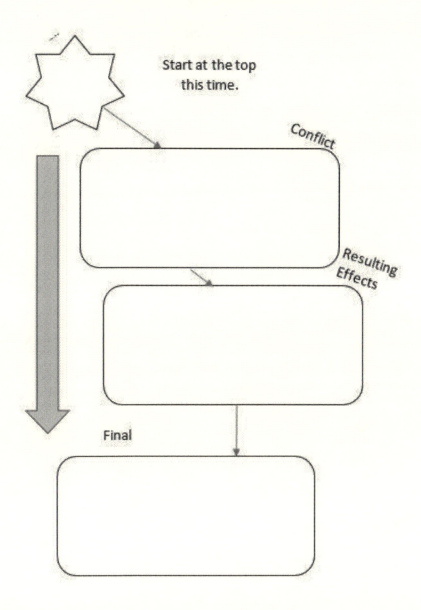

Resolution

It's all downhill after the climax. The night crew arrives to mop up loose ends and explain anything that may have been lost in the storytelling. If you do this correctly, you won't need an epilogue. If you want to use the technical term, denouement, for the untying of all the complex plot steps, feel free.

Your characters are in a "new normal" from the experiences and journeys you put them through and the reader might feel a sense of catharsis at this point as well.

Is it ok to not tie up every loose end? Of course it is. If you're writing a serial, you'll want to make sure that there is a tie-in to the next book as well as clues and details in Book One that are critical in Book Two. Not every loose end has the same weight either. That lost dog on page 78? Your reader may not need to know he was found by his owner at the end (unless it's critical to your story).

Exercise: *Think About It*

The critical question here is:

Exactly what details does your reader need closure on?

List them below.

The B Story

What's the B story?

Often called a subplot, it can be the supporting storyline that reinforces your theme and gives you another way to reinforce the main story. It runs parallel to the A (the main plot) and acts like a mirror. If your hero is a failure in the A story, the B story can show her having some success. It supports the main story and provides insight to the readers. In a well-written story, the A storyline and B storyline merge together for the final crisis with the B story providing critical information for the resolution.

The best way to explain it is with an example from Peter Pan.

The main story: An eternal boy takes children to a magical island where they decide to return home and grow up after all.

The B story: Tinkerbell is jealous of Wendy

Crisis: Tinkerbell faces her jealously and helps save Peter Pan, Wendy, and the Lost Boys

Can you think of other examples?

The main story:

The B story:

Crisis:

The main story:

The B story:

Crisis:

If you're having trouble identifying them, watch a couple of movies and see if you can identify the A and B storylines. Most modern American movies use this strategy.

FIVE MINUTES TO SUCCESS

Exercise: Think About Your Own Story

The main story:

The B story:

Crisis:

The Three Act Model

Pacing (how fast or slow the story is revealed) requires a bit of mastery to avoid the midbook drag. It keeps the reader turning pages using rhythm, sense of time, and word choice. It requires deciding where plot points have to occur and what leads up to the next major conflict.

One helpful technique is to use the Three Act Model. It assists in charting the timing of the plot points as well as figuring out if your story is on pace. While used more frequently in screenwriting, it is useful in novel writing as well.

There are three Acts-- the beginning and end Acts are shorter while the middle Act has the meat of the story in it. The chart below shows you that the Act ends with a Major Conflict/plot point. There are other setbacks, obstacles, minor conflicts, and failures but most of those are in Act Two.

Act 1: The Set Up (25% of the total pages)

Inciting Incident

Beginning of the journey

First Major Conflict

Act 2: The Confrontations (50% of the total pages)

Minor Setbacks/Roadblocks

Minor Conflict

Midpoint Twist (halfway through)

More Obstacles

More Failure

More Conflicts

Major Conflict

Act 3: Resolution (25% of the total pages)

Climax

Resolution

Exercise: *Your Turn*

Have you broken your work down like this? Why not try it and see what it reveals to you. If you're in the editing process and someone has said the middle drags, use this tool to diagnose the problem.

Act 1: The Set Up (page count: 1 to ___)

Inciting Incident

Beginning of the journey

First Major Conflict

Act 2: The Confrontations (page count: ___ to ___)

Minor Setbacks/Roadblocks

Minor Conflict

Midpoint Twist (halfway page number ___)

More Obstacles

More Failure

More Conflicts

Major Conflict

Five Minutes to Success

Act 3: Resolution (page count: ____ to _____)

Climax

Resolution

Part 2
The Art of the Edit

What's Next? The Editing Process

And now you've done it. You've followed all the advice in the story crafting section and written a novel. Or a short story. Or a novella. Whatever you wrote, it's perfect, and now it's time to spew it out into the world and wait for the wheelbarrows of money to show up at your doorstep.

Or maybe not.

Did you edit it?

Did you edit it again?

Did you get it beta read, consider your readers' feedback, rewrite it, and edit it again?

No?

Then don't do anything else until you've read the next sections. We're going to talk about some self-editing strategies to make sure your work is something you'll be proud to share with the world.

Mastering the Craft of Writing

The Sucky First Draft

Maybe you're ahead of the game. Maybe you've picked up this book in anticipation of finishing your first novel, but it's not done yet. Half-finished. Not even started.

Here's the best advice I can give you: Write the words. Just write. Get the story out. Finish it. Don't worry if you haven't weaved in all the symbolism you intended, or if you haven't described your magic system fully, or if your main character is lifeless and flat. Don't worry about grammar or formatting or punctuation. Just write the words. Tell the story.

Because here's the big secret. All first drafts suck.

That's what they're supposed to do. They're a framework. The bare essentials of your story. The empty walls upon which you must now go back and spread the paint, mount the shelves, and hang the pictures. Sometimes you realize what you actually need to do is knock out a few walls and add a sunroom. That's fine, too. But start with your frame. You can't make it better until it exists.

I'm sure there are some folks out there who poop out beautiful first drafts. As the words fly from their fingers, they're accompanied by a perfect spattering of commas, and all the right dialog tags. But you know what? I don't care. It doesn't matter. Whether you labor over every semicolon now, slowing down the creative flow of the story and miring yourself in minutiae, or whether you just barf it onto the page and fix it later, I will never know. As long as you edit properly, it doesn't matter one bit how awful your first draft was.

Every book you've ever read has been rewritten multiple times.

Between self-edits and rewrites, beta reader suggestions, agent and editor corrections, and just plain re-thinkings of the story, there isn't one professionally published work out there that is the result of a writer pooping out a story, typing, "The End," and sending it right to the bookstore shelves. Writing is rewriting. Get used to it. There will be changes. This is a good thing. But to change a thing, you've got to have a thing, so write the thing.

I use a code when I write. It's AAAA. This is a searchable "word" that I use whenever I know I'm writing something that needs fixing but I don't want to stop my flow to do it right now. Sometimes that manifests as, "I know this is a horrible line of dialog, but I'll fix it later. Gotta get on with the story." Other times it's because I need to research something, but I know that if I stop right now and start looking online for the proper hierarchy of honeybee hives, I'm going to end up down the rabbit hole. Three hours later I'll be reading an article about the history of Notre Dame football, and I won't have written a single word. So instead, I'll write, "The drone bee AAAA buzzed around a rosebush." It might not be the drones that go out looking for honey. I don't know. And right now, I don't care.

Mastering the Craft of Writing

I make the note so I can go back later, do the research, and fix it. But right now I'm writing my story.

If you haven't finished your draft yet, just take a deep breath and write. Don't worry about perfect. Don't worry about beautiful. Just make your story exist.

Five Minutes to Success

Exercise: Think About It

Are you putting off finishing your story because you're trying to make it perfect on the first draft?

Have you ever set aside a story because you got bogged down on details or lost the flow before it was done?

What roadblocks have kept you from finishing a work?

What's Next After Your First Draft is Complete?

First, CELEBRATE! You have accomplished something major! It's said that over 80% of people want to write a book, but that only 1% finish one. You are now a member of the One Percent Club! Great job! We are thrilled for you-- seriously! It took some serious self-discipline and sacrifice to get this place.

But you're not going to like our next advice.

Set it aside.

What?

Why?

Save it someplace safe and let it age like a fine wine.

You have lived with this project for an extensive period of time. It's in your mind, your dreams, your conversations. It has soaked into your skin and you need to be able to look at it from a fresh point of view in order to edit it. For as long as possible. Until you're not thinking about it. Jeri suggests 6 months if you've invested more than a year while Wendy is fine with a month or two. Don't rush this process simply because you want a book with your name on the cover in print in time for the Christmas sales.

What do you do next?

Write another book. We strongly suggest that even if you're self-publishing that you don't start Book 2 of a series while Book 1 is resting. Take notes, do your pre-writing, plotting, character studies, but there is a huge chance that Book 1 will change so much during the editing process that you'll waste of your work on Book 2 if you do it now. This is a great time to write short stories for anthologies, read books you've not had time to read, or explore that niblet of an idea that you keep suppressing.

Or

Try some of these other things you've not done yet.

Build your Writer's Platform (twitter, Facebook, Goodreads, Instagram, website). There is more about it in the section about Selling Your Book.

Hang out on social media with groups that kin to the topics/themes in your book.

Build an online following. "But, Jeri," you say, "I don't have a book yet. It's not even been through round one of editing."

Look into the future with me. It's Launch Day. Who's buying your book? Your mom, your sister, your best friend?

Hear the sound of the dust swirling in the desert? That's the sound of NO SALES!

This is the time to identify your people, your tribe, those who want to read your book if they knew it existed. Once you find them, be part of their community. Not so that they'll buy your book, but because giving back is part of you are as human being.

Be a cheerleader and an encourager, a sharer of information, someone who cares about others. I belong to a community where we love a specific toy (not because they show up in my books, but because I love this little expensive toy) and a mom shared about how her autistic daughter loved these little things and she needed help finding cheap ones. Our group sent that child these things until she was overwhelmed. I may never sell a book to that group, but I made a kid happy with a box in her mailbox. That's what being a part of a community looks like at times.

Participate in online and face-to-face writer groups. Listen more than you talk and learn everything you can. Ask questions, even if they sound dumb. We all had those same questions until someone answered them for us. Don't bring your work to a new group until you know they are going to be serious about improving your skills as a writer. Not all groups are the same. The one Wendy and I go to focuses on making each work shine. We're not there to say, "Well, look at that! You put a whole bunch of words on a page!" as Wendy often says to our new members. You have people for that. We're there to tell you if you accomplished your goal and how to improve your craft. Many of our first timers don't come back because we don't tell them what they want to hear. It's never about the writer though. It's always 100% about learning the craft so the work will sing with happiness when you release it.

Exercise: Think About It

Why is it hard for authors to follow this advice?

What is your plan of action for the time between finishing a book and starting to edit it?

Who are your people, the ones dying to read this book? Where do they hang out and how can you access them in a non-creepy manner?

Manuscript Format

Our critique group examines ten pages of a work at a time and we ask for the work to be in manuscript form. Unlike what some authors think, that doesn't mean ready for publication. Rather, it means your manuscript should be formatted in the typical expectations of publishers. It's fairly simple:

12-point font

Usually boring old Times New Roman

Double spaced

Page numbers

A header with the title and author's name

Why? Because it's easier to read for the person reviewing the work, leaves plenty of white space for comments and suggestions, and it's a sign that you know what publishers expect. It is a way of treating your work with respect as well.

We hear people talking about breaking the rules in writing, and this is one of those places where rule breaking happens. If you decide you're not using the expected format, please make sure that it moves your story forward and isn't because you like the color purple or the happy little flowers the font makes when you write certain letters. When a publisher looks at your work, they'll be evaluating it from a professional, business point of view. You don't want it rejected because it'll cost too much to print or isn't professional enough for their company.

Why Grammar Matters

I know a lot of writers. Between my in-person writing group and the online groups I belong to, I see a lot of new writers' work. Time and again they've said it. "Punctuation and grammar don't really matter because my editor will fix it for me." They don't want to bother learning comma rules or how to properly use quotation marks. They aren't worried about splices or misplaced modifiers because some magical person is going to come along after them and *BibbidiBobbidiBoo* their words into a readable format.

It's not going to happen.

Agents and editors won't read past page one if it's filled with grammar mistakes. No matter how spectacular your story might be, they'll never find out because they'll never read it.

It's like this. My husband is a chef. One of the things he does in the summer is judging at the county fair. Cakes, candy, fudge, cookies... he's the guy handing out the blue ribbons. I watched him judge once. He stood behind a counter upon which were lined up about twenty-five plates of peanut butter fudge. Can you imagine tasting twenty-five bites of peanut butter fudge and choosing a winner? You might think you can, but trust me, after about ten bites your tongue will be a dried-up fungus, immune to the taste of sugar for days. So how does he do it? Here's the secret: he doesn't taste them all. The first thing he does is walk down the row with a knife, smooshing one piece of fudge on each plate, looking at the texture. Grainy? Crystals? Not uniform through the piece? Automatic disqualification. By the time he's ruled out the ones with obvious visual flaws, he only has to taste maybe ten bites to choose a winner. That's hard, but possible. And that's what agents and editors are doing. From the hundreds of submissions, they're tossing out the ones with obvious errors so they only have to read the ones that might have a shot at winning. "But Wendy," you say. "That's so unfair." Maybe it is. But it's true, and you can either believe me and have a shot, or ignore me and wonder why your pile of form rejection letters is taller than you are.

Readers are exactly the same way. If you plan to self-publish, you might think it's not as important. "Readers don't care," you'll say. "They don't know grammar any better than I do. It's all about the story." Yes, they do. And no, it's not. They might not be able to tell you why a dependent clause is offensive as a sentence fragment, but they'll know it grates on their eyeballs. They might buy your first novel if it's $0.99 e-book, but they'll never buy another. And that will be the end of your writing career.

"That's okay," you say. "I'll pay a professional editor." If you plan to self-publish, that's the smartest thing you've said all day. Ditto if you're rotten at grammar but want to find a publisher. But guess what? Most editors will ask to see a sample of your work before they'll take you on as a client. If they see that your work is a mess and their job is going to be a grueling slog, they'll charge you more. Some will refuse you outright.

Everyone needs editing help. It's a known fact that the human brain has a hard time seeing its own mistakes. I have looked at the same typo ten times in a manuscript and never noticed it, because I'm the one who typed it. I'm pretty good at grammar, but I would never publish a book that didn't have another person's eyes to proofread it. No one can find all their own errors, and while a few tiny mistakes here and there won't sink your chances with an agent or reader, having the most perfect, polished manuscript ensures that whoever is reading it won't get hung up in all your grammatical disasters and leave your story halfway through. Smooth, error-free writing allows the reader to focus on the story. And isn't that why you're writing?

Five Minutes to Success

Exercise: Review

What are the main points of this section?

Why are they critical?

Do you agree or disagree with them?

Adverbs

Listen up, I do beseech, this tale of woe devised,

To tell about a part of speech maligned and much despised.

The lowly adverb, I suggest, has earned the writers' scoff

For lazy authors, so distressed when editors scratch off.

They tell the place, the time, the way, perhaps the frequency;

describe the verb and thus portray the manner or degree.

But lest ye fall to ink of red, pay heed to this advice:

When adverbs do the work instead, your verbs may not suffice.

--D.W. Vogel

There is no more discussed part of speech among writers than the lowly adverb. Passions run high when they start popping up like dandelions on the golf course. Every writer has heard about how evil they are, and how their very soul risks eternal damnation if they don't search each document for the hated -LY and cut them all.

I am not an adverb purist. They have their place, as do all parts of speech. But to use them correctly, you must understand them, treacherous little beasts that they are.

Adverbs are like viruses. Most of the time when you get a virus, you get sick. A head full of snot and a throat full of goop, or a lip covered in cold sores. Viruses are not our friends. But some viruses live in our guts and protect us from virulent bacteria that want to ruin your next airline flight or long business meeting. Some of them teach your immune system how to fight off other, more dangerous invaders. Still others live in the fungus that live in the plants that grow around geysers in soil too hot for regular plants to grow. Mostly viruses are bad. But in the right place and time, they can save your life. Especially if you're a geyser-loving fungus.

So what are they?

Adverbs are words that modify a verb. They can also modify adjectives and other adverbs.

The simplest ones are the ones that end in -ly. Most of these are adverbs of manner, telling how something was done. I walked slowly. She chews loudly. These are the bad adverbs, and we'll talk about why in the next section.

Others are adverbs of time, place, frequency, or degree.

These are all adverbs: always, sometimes, soon, so far, here, everywhere, above, inside, almost, enough, never, seldom, again.

Those aren't what you think of when you think "adverb" are they? But they are. They still describe the verb they're used with.

As a general rule, those adverbs are pretty okay. This is because they're usually necessary for the sentence to make sense. You should be aware of them in your writing, but the great red pen of death doesn't have to descend on any adverb that can't be replaced by using a stronger verb.

Five Minutes to Success

Exercise: Practice

Pick out the adverbs in these sentences.

Mary never picks me up from school anymore. (This one is tricky...there are two)

I like camping, but Jack prefers to sleep inside.

Susan was so happy to get a puppy. (Also tricky because the adverb here isn't modifying a verb. It's modifying an adjective.)

Adverbs of Manner

These are the bad guys. Adverbs of manner describe how something is done, and most of the time they're used because a weak verb isn't carrying its weight.

Like this:

I walked slowly and quietly into the room.

Grammatically this sentence is correct. But "walked" is a weak verb. If we replace it with a stronger verb we get:

I crept into the room.

BOOM! No adverbs needed! When your verb is doing the work, it doesn't need a bunch of adverbs to tell your reader how something is happening. And that's why editors hate them so much. In most cases, those -ly adverbs indicate a weak verb. And that indicates a weak writer, or at least a writer who didn't edit well enough.

Let's look at a few more examples.

Casey sat dejectedly in the chair.

-or-

Casey slumped in the chair.

A song was played repeatedly on the radio.

-or-

The radio repeated the same song. (This ditches the adverb AND the passive voice. Win/win!)

And a longer bit here:

She walked slowly down the rows of cages. Dogs sat sadly in some; in others they barked loudly, jumping excitedly at the chain link doors. Finally, she stopped. In the last run, an old beagle sat morosely on a dirty blanket. It looked hopelessly into her eyes. "That's the one," she said quietly. "That's the dog for me."

-or-

She padded down the rows of cages. Each one held a dog; some cowering in the back, and others yapping and lunging at the chain link doors. She stopped. In the last run, and old beagle huddled on a dirty blanket. Its hopeless eyes met hers. "That's the one," she whispered. "That's the dog for me."

No one is saying you have to purge every single adverb from your work. The writing muses will not forsake you if a few slip past, even if they are of the dreaded -ly variety. But if your writing is peppered with them, you're not going to get very far. Agents and editors look for excessive adverb use as a sign of weak, lazy writing. Readers get fatigued from endless descriptive adverb use. If you're going to use them, all I ask is that you be aware of it. Do a search on your writing software for "ly" and consider each one. Is it necessary? Can you use a stronger verb and eliminate the need for it? If you drop it out of the sentence, will you lose anything? If the adverb is pulling its weight, it can stay. But most of them are just a crutch for a weak verb.

Five Minutes to Success

Exercise: Practice

Rewrite these sentences to eliminate the adverbs.

She happily accepted his proposal.

The boys jumped eagerly into the truck and drove quickly away.

"I don't want to go," she said sadly. "Nobody likes me there." (Hint: try an action tag for this one)

Point of View

Folks get confused about point of view (POV). We talked earlier about the three basic kinds of narration: First Person, Third Person Limited, and Third Person Omniscient. We mentioned Second Person (you, as in: You walk down the hall. You open the door...generally only used in "Choose You Own Adventure" types of books). Now it's time to delve into how point of view changes in each of these narrations.

First person is simple. If you're writing in first person, think of your writing as a diary. You're writing as if you are the main character, recounting the story that happened (or is happening, depending on the tense you choose) to you. As in: I always wanted to be a painter. So when I got the opportunity to study art in Paris, I packed my bags and shouted, "Au revoir!" That's first person. I never studied art in Paris, but my first person narrator did, so I write as if it's me. That's why the point of view is simple.

If I'm writing a first person scene where I'm talking to my art teacher, I can only know what's in my own head. I can't read minds (unless you're writing a telepathic fantasy, in which case all POV bets are off). Look at this little scene:

"I'm really excited to be learning from such a great teacher," I said. "I can't wait to start doing oil paintings."

My teacher was disappointed. "I teach sculpture, not painting."

What's wrong with that exchange? I can't know that my teacher is disappointed. I'm not a mind reader. I might see her frown, or her shoulders sag. She might sigh, or shake her head. I might guess that she's disappointed, but I cannot possibly know for sure what she's feeling because I am not in her point of view. So I can't say how she felt. Those kinds of POV errors, when a non-POV character's inner thoughts are stated as fact by the POV character, are the insidious "head hop" of first person.

Head hopping

I've mentioned this Bad Thing before, and it's time to talk about it.

The best way to describe it is to talk about filming a movie.

If you filmed a movie in first person, there would be one single camera. It would literally be the eyes of the narrator. The camera would always be looking out from one person's perspective. It's very hard to pull off in film. *Being John Malkovitch* had some great first person scenes, and *Cloverfield* used a single camera view, though the camera could be handed from person to person, so wasn't strictly first person perspective. But when you think about filming a movie through one person's eyes, you can imagine the POV. Never a top-down view. Never a view of the narrator except in a mirror (which is a big first person cliché). Never from anyone else's point of view. If the narrator doesn't know it, the reader doesn't know it.

Third person is a bit trickier

The movie cameras in third person can be anywhere in the room filming the action. But when you get too many cameras pointing in too many directions, things get chaotic.

Let's look at an iconic movie scene, the Cantina at Mos Eisley in *Star Wars* Episode Four. There are a lot of people in that scene. Aliens, humans, bartenders, musicians. If we tried to see that scene through all their eyes, we'd throw up from all the camera jumps. We see a lot, but there are really only two points of view: Luke and Han Solo. All the opening shots of the interior are Luke's POV. We see what he's seeing as he walks in. We also see him walking in, because this is third person, not first. We hear the music he hears, and we watch him belly up to the bar.

POV shift. Now we're at a table watching Han Solo negotiate with Greedo. Although there are multiple camera angles, this is Han's scene. He shoots (first), and we're back to Luke. Obi-Wan is there, and Chewbacca is there, but we never see them by themselves. The scene is easy to follow because we aren't jumping around from character to character.

Here are some general rules for third person limited:

Use the fewest points of view possible to tell your story. If you have a lot, consider whether you can tell some scenes from other characters' POVs to streamline the narration. If you have more than four or five POVs, you probably have too many (remember the end of the Lord of the Rings movies? All those endings that dragged on for an hour after the movie should have ended? That's because there were so many POV characters in those books).

Use one single POV per section. If possible, make that "section" be "chapter", but if you have to have multiple POVs in a chapter, separate each character's POV scene by a scene break...skipped lines, or *** with skipped lines. If you don't, that's head hopping... jumping from one character's POV (with their inner thoughts available) into another's without a break. This robs your scene of focus and makes your reader dizzy. Readers who aren't also writers may not realize why they're having trouble connecting with your characters, but head hopping is a great way to do that.

We may only know the inner thoughts of the current POV character. If it's a John POV scene, we can't know that Mary is regretting her decision. John can observe her expression, or assume she's feeling regretful, but the reader cannot know Mary's thoughts.

A lot of novice writers want to write in third person omniscient. They think that an omniscient narrator will allow them to show their reader what every character is doing and thinking, and this will make the storytelling easier. But omniscient is rare in modern literature, and few writers pull it off well. Those that do are often humor writers like Douglas Adams and Sir Terry Pratchett, who use the omniscient narrator to fill in the funny bits that their characters wouldn't think about.

A good omniscient narrator is just that...a narrator. The old-fashioned children's book style of, "Let me tell you a story about two children who learned an important lesson about witches and candy houses," is omniscient. It's a person sitting by a fire telling a tale. The narrator, while not a character in the story, has a distinct voice and opinions to share. If you find yourself using phrases like, "Little did he know his life was about to change," you're writing in omniscient. But like I said, it's not popular right now, and it's tremendously difficult to do well. First time writers rarely do it well.

The reason it's so hard to pull off is distance. An omniscient narrator knows everyone's thoughts, and by sharing them all instead of focusing on a few POV characters, dilutes the close connection of reader to main character. It's a lot more exciting to watch dinosaurs chase people through the jungle than it is to watch me telling you about dinosaurs chasing people through the jungle.

In general, if the only reason you're using an omniscient narrator is because you think you need to show us the inner thoughts of all your characters, I urge you to consider rewriting with a couple of strong, limited POV characters. Lack of connection to the main character is a huge reason why people give up on books in the early chapters. Hooking readers into your story is a difficult course to run. Don't tie your shoelaces together without a darned good reason.

Exercise: *Think About It*

Go to library and pick up a stack of books (from your genre). See if you can identify the POV shifts in each book.

What did you learn? What information is "new to you"? What impact will it have on your writing?

FIVE MINUTES TO SUCCESS

The Sentence

The sentence is the atom of the story world. It's the basic building block from which the story itself is made. While the words are the subatomic particles, zipping around and doing their electron dance, the structure of your sentences is what makes you story sing.

So what is a sentence?

At its simplest, it's a subject and a verb.

Harry cried. I went. Sandy limped.

The subject and the verb must agree in number. You don't say "Harry cry." The verb tense must agree with the rest of the story. So that's really all you need to have a sentence.

Things get more complicated after that.

As you start to expand your sentences into clauses, you'll have to start looking for the sneaky fragments that will hide in your work, pretending to be something they're not. You'll have to watch for the dangling modifiers, unclear antecedents, and the subject/verb disagreements that can turn your story into a war zone. We'll talk about all these in the next sections.

For now, let's talk about sentence structure in general. One of the most common mistakes I see when I'm editing is repeated sentence structure. You'll find one you like, and just keep doing it.

Like this:

Stopping the car, Jerry jumped out. Reaching for his keys, he dashed to the front door. Jamming the key in the lock, he was shocked to find the door unlatched.

It's usually not that obvious...not three in a row exactly the same. But you wouldn't want to see those three sentences together in a paragraph of five sentences. It's monotonous.

The best writing uses variance of sentence structure for pace and emphasis. If you're writing about a languid day on the beach, you might choose to use longer descriptive sentences. You can linger on your words, even in your dialog. The sentences take time, and we have plenty of it on this lazy summer day. The paragraphs can be longer and the action slower. Nobody's in any kind of hurry.

Then we see the sharks.

Now things are moving. People are running, screaming. They're shouting for their kids to get out of the water. Lifeguards scramble to rescue panicked swimmers. The sharks get closer.

See what I did there? I used sentence structure for pace and emphasis. The pace shows in the length of the sentences. In the first part they're longer, more meandering. The structure is a bit more complex, which slows you down.

Then you saw the sharks.

See how I set that off in its own paragraph? See how it's a short, clipped sentence all by itself? Of course you do. I wanted you to see it. I wanted you to be drifting along on that lazy summer day, dreaming in the sunshine, and then WHAM. SHARKS. I wanted you to pull up short. No way to miss it. And did you notice that I didn't have to use the word "suddenly"? That's a horrible word in writing because it's nearly always unnecessary. I showed you it was sudden by using the short sentence all alone in its own paragraph. The white space around it drew your eye and slammed your sunbathing to a nasty, sharky halt. Then I kept the pace moving in the next paragraph with more short sentences, all with simple structures. Those draw your eye forward at a fast clip. Just reading the words gets quicker.

Literary fiction is all about the loveliness of its sentences, but even if you're not writing literary, you should always be paying attention to your structure and how you could be using the sentences themselves, not just the words that make them up, to lead readers where you want them to go.

Mastering the Craft of Writing

Exercise: Think About It

What kind of sentence structure would you use to describe a spooky old castle?

What kind to describe a space shuttle launch?

Misplaced Modifiers

These are my favorite mistakes, because they're so often hilarious.

Like this:

Bending down for the dropped syringe, his eyes followed the nurse's every move.

In this sentence, the participle phrase (Bending down for the dropped syringe) is closest to the subject "his eyes." So it's saying that his eyes were bending over to pick up the syringe. Ouch.

Here's another:

Betsy wanted to wear her brand-new dress to the dance, which was unfortunately stained from a coffee spill.

In this sentence, we're saying that the dance was stained, not the dress. That would take a lot of coffee.

To fix them, we just have to move them around.

His eyes followed the nurse's every move as she bent down for the dropped syringe.

Betsy wanted to wear her brand-new dress to the dance, but it was unfortunately stained from a coffee spill.

We see the same issue with pronouns.

Read this sentence:

The picture frame on the shelf fell over, damaging it.

What got damaged here? The frame or the shelf? You can't tell because it's unclear.

Here's another:

Betsy surprised her mother by pouring coffee on her dress.

Whose dress has the coffee stain now? It could be Betsy or her mom.

These unclear pronouns are sneaky, especially when you have a scene with multiple people of the same gender. If you have four men in the room and you start saying things like, "He talked to him about his car," we're not going to know who HE and HIM are, nor whose car is being discussed. It's a time for greater reliance on names, and the use of action tags so we know who's doing what without you having to write, "John said," and "Rob said," a hundred times.

Five Minutes to Success

Exercise: Practice

Fix these misplaced modifiers.

Petting my cat, she purred on my lap.

The loud explosions vibrated the windows, which were giving him a headache.

Subject/Verb Agreement

These are easy to mess up. Your subject must agree with your verb in number. That seems simple, but it can trip you up when you use words like all or some, everyone and someone.

Here's an example:

All of the students have gone home.

All of the milk has been spilled.

Both of those sentences are correct, but in the first one "all" is plural because "students" is plural, and in the second "milk" is singular.

Everyone, nobody, and someone are always singular.

Everyone has gone to the moon.

Nobody is listening anymore.

The words "neither" and "either" will mess you up as well. They always require a singular verb even though they're used to talk about more than one thing.

Like this:

Neither of us is going to give in.

Either Mary or Jane could win the game.

But then there's this rule to consider. When you're using "either" or "neither" with an "or" between them, and the two things you're describing differ in number, the verb has to agree with whichever one it's closer to.

Like this:

Either my husband or my brothers are going to pick me up.

In this case we use the plural "are" because the closest subject (my brothers) is plural.

If we turned it around, it would be:

Either my brothers or my husband is going to pick me up.

If you're stumped by these, try removing the "Either BLANK or" from the sentence. You wouldn't say, "My brothers is going to pick me up," nor would you say, "My husband are going to pick me up." When you're baffled by verb agreement, remove as much as you can from the sentence and try to get yourself down to the barest subject and verb.

The last stumper is "as well as" and "along with." It will mess you up because it's not the same as "and" for making subjects plural.

Like this:

My husband along with my brothers is going to pick me up.

My husband and my brothers are going to pick me up.

Both of these are correct. When you use "along with," the subject remains "my husband". He's still singular. But when you switch it to "and", now it's plural.

The good news is that modern editing software will find a lot of these errors for you. It's always best for you to know the rules so you can avoid making the mistakes in the first place.

Five Minutes to Success

Exercise: Practice

Which of these sentences are correct? (Oh, that's a tricky one there, but I just gave you a hint. If I'd said, "Which of these sentences IS correct, you'd know there was only one. Since I said, "Which ARE correct," you know you're looking for more than one. Sneaky verbs.)

Mary as well as her dogs is going to enjoy the park.

Neither Mary nor her dogs are going to enjoy the park.

The room was full of students, and everyone was enjoying the show.

Pronoun/Antecedent Agreement

That just sounds scary, doesn't it? Don't be alarmed. It's not as bad as it sounds.

Pronoun/Antecedent agreement means that when you're using a pronoun, it has to agree in number with the thing it's being used in place of.

Here's an example:

I'm writing this book so that a reader can learn from it and improve their writing.

That's a tricky one. It's wrong because "reader" is singular and "their" is plural. People mess this up all the time because of gender confusion. I don't know if the reader I'm talking about is male or female, so I can't say that I want my reader to improve his writing. Technically it should be "his or her" writing, but that gets ungainly, and fast. I try to avoid these in my writing whenever possible. If I were using that sentence, I'd change it to this:

I'm writing this book so that readers can learn from it and improve their writing.

Problem solved.

The other pronoun issue you'll see is when you're compounding your pronoun with something else.

Like this:

Five Minutes to Success

The award was for Sarah and me.

That's correct, but a lot of people might write it as, "Sarah and I." But break the sentence down. Get rid of Sarah (I never liked her anyway). Now it's just: The award was for me. You wouldn't say the award was for I.

Here's another one:

Me and Josie are heading out for a snack.

It's wrong because you wouldn't say: Me are heading out for a snack. You wouldn't even say: Me is heading out for a snack. That's caveman talk. But it looks weird to write: I and Josie are heading out for a snack. It's correct, but it's ugly. Switch it around and say: Josie and I are heading out for a snack. As a side note, I would absolutely use a line like, "Me and Josie are heading out," in dialog, because it's how people talk. But talking isn't the same as writing. Sorting that out is the key to believable dialog.

Mastering the Craft of Writing

Exercise: Practice

Fix these sentences:

One of the children ate their sandwich too fast and choked.

She hoped someone would find the letter and their heart would be healed by the words.

Filtering

One of the first pieces of advice I received on my writing came from an editor at a mid-size publisher who was considering one of my manuscripts. The book didn't make the cut (because they are a romance publisher, and apparently without the "Happily Ever After" ending, it's not really a romance, but that's another story...literally), but the couple of R and R's (Revise and Resubmits) I got were full of excellent advice from a professional editor.

The first thing she taught me to cut was filtering.

What's filtering? Filtering is when you show the things that are happening in a scene by having a character experience it. Filtering is, "He saw," "She heard," "I smelled," "I noticed." Writers often use these filters because they're trying to keep the action centered around their character, but what it actually does is distance the reader from the action. Instead of seeing a beautiful sunset, I'm watching Lauren see a beautiful sunset. I don't smell the rotting fruit in the trash, I watch Ellen smell it. It puts one more layer of sense between the reader and the action, and that's never good.

Here's an example:

Rachel turned around. She saw the door swing open and heard the creak of its hinges. She felt an icy chill run down her back. "How...how did you find me?" Rachel watched in horror as her ex-husband stepped through the door. The room was dark, but there was enough light for her to see the glint off the blade of his knife.

Okay, that's grammatically correct. It's readable. But did it make you feel anything? Probably not.

Let's try this:

Rachel turned around. The door swung open with an audible creak from its old hinges. An icy chill ran down her back. "How...how did you find me?" Her ex-husband stepped through the door. Even in the dark room, his knife blade glinted.

Did you feel anything that time? If you did, it's because I removed the filtering. Instead of seeing Rachel's reactions to things, you get to react to them yourself. The very occasional filter won't sink your manuscript, but if you're starting to submit stories and novels and getting a lot of comments like, "Not bad, but I just couldn't connect with your main character," you might be a victim of filtering. Go through and look for all those sensory words, and cut as many as you can.

Five Minutes to Success

Exercise: Practice

Rewrite these sentences to remove the filters.

Jerry smelled bacon frying in the kitchen.

Sandra heard birds singing outside her window.

Peering through the porthole, I saw the storm approaching our ship.

Expletives

No, I don't mean curse words. The need to cut expletives from my writing was the second thing that wonderful editor taught me. What are expletives?

Expletives are when you use an "it" or a "there" that doesn't directly refer to anything. They usually come at the beginnings of sentences, and they look like this:

It is the secretary's job to keep the minutes.

What does that "It" refer to? Nothing. You can drop it and say: The secretary's job is to keep the minutes. That "It" doesn't belong.

Here's another:

There was no chance for Earl to win the title.

What's that "There" doing? Nothing. Fix it and make it more concise: Earl had no chance to win the title. It's cleaner and tighter, and that's what makes contemporary publishing happy.

The very worst offender is:

It was then that they realized he wasn't coming.

Oh, sweet Charlotte, that's a bad one. It's an expletive and a "then." If we fix it, we get: They realized he wasn't coming. So much stronger.

Five Minutes to Success

Look through your writing for sentences that start with "It" and "There." If you can cut them and not lose meaning, those are expletives, and they have to go.

Exercise: Practice

Fix these expletive sentences.

It was never my intention to hurt you.

There was always a chance he would reconsider.

It was not until they heard his car that they really believed he was coming home.

Useless Words Must Die

Useless words abound in our language, and they're trying so hard to sneak into your manuscript. They weaken your writing and slow down your reader, but because they're common in everyday speech, they're hard to find.

Here's a list of words and phrases that rarely pull their weight:

Very, Actually, So, Just, Then, Really, Literally, A lot, So as to, Start, Begin

None of these are bad words. And I can hear you from way over there. "But Wendy," you say. "You start half the sentences in this book with 'So'." You're right, I do. But this isn't fiction. This is an advice book, and it's written blog-style, which is casual and chatty. So has a place here.

But look at this sentence.

She was so happy to hear the good news.

If we remove the SO, what do we lose? Nothing. She was happy to hear the good news. And I'd argue that "happy" should probably go, too, because it's weak. She was ecstatic, or overjoyed, or pleased. Each of those has its own connotation, and they all say more than "happy" does.

More examples:

I really want you to come along. ...If we lose the "really," what do we lose?"

Mastering the Craft of Writing

She loved him a lot. ...Boring.

I went into my bedroom, then I sat on the edge of my bed. ..."Then" is usually useless. Do a search for it and you'll be shocked how often it's doing nothing but cluttering up your sentences. Unless you're writing a time travel book, things only happen in one order. You don't need to tell me something happened, THEN something else happened.

He studied hard so as to make sure he got into a good school. ...Cut the "so as" and we have: He studied hard to make sure he got into a good school. We lose nothing except two useless words.

She began to dance. ...This one is a bit trickier, but as a general rule, you should only say that someone began to do something if they were prevented from actually doing it. How do you begin to dance? You don't. You just dance. If you begin to dance but stop before you make a move, I want to see you raise your hands or jiggle your butt to the beat or something.

Five Minutes to Success

Exercise: Practice

Cut the useless words from these sentences.

Janice was very upset when she saw the news report. (Hint: can you find a single word that means "very upset" and will strengthen the sentence?)

I actually like doing homework.

Terry wanted to go see a movie, so he got in the car and then turned the key in the ignition.

Punctuation in Dialog

There are so many places you can go wrong with dialog. We'll talk in a later chapter about what makes dialog good or bad, and when you should use it to propel your story. But first let's talk about the nuts and bolts of putting those lines on the page.

Dialog is surrounded by quotation marks. There are no spaces between the quotes and the dialog itself.

Like this: "I want to go to the market today." Easy enough.

When you add in a dialog tag, the quotes go after the comma that sets it off. "I want to go to the market today," Jane said. It's the same if there's a period, a question mark, or an exclamation mark at the end of the dialog. "I want to go to the market today!" Jane yelled, or "Do you want to go to the market today?" Jane asked. If the dialog tag is first, the quotes go after the comma, as in: Jane said, "I want to go to the market today."

Or if you're using an action tag instead, it goes after the period. "I want to go to the market today." Jane stomped her foot.

Even if you're breaking up the dialog with your tag, the rules are the same. "I want to go the market today," Jane said, "because I need to buy apples for a pie."

Things start to get really dicey when you're putting quotes within quotes. Like this: John said, "I love reading Shakespeare. My favorite quote is, 'Love all, trust a few, do wrong to none.'"

We open the dialog with opening double quotation marks, then when the Shakespeare quote starts we put that into single quotation marks (if it didn't appear in dialog, the Shakespeare quote would be in double quotation marks. But you can't have doubles inside doubles. Only singles go inside doubles.). At the end, we have to close the singles around the quote, and the doubles around the dialog.

The other trick is that if you're writing a long speech and you want to break it up into multiple paragraphs as the person keeps talking, you don't close the quotes at the end of the first paragraph, but you DO open them in the next one. That rule is odd, but it's how you do it.

Like this:

John looked out over the crowd. "Today is a historic day, my friends. We're embarking on a great voyage. This spaceship, the result of a cooperation among nations never seen before, will carry the seeds of the human race across the galaxy. The descendants of the lucky passengers who leave our doomed planet will someday arrive on a new world.

"We don't know what they will find there. We only know this: with them go the hopes of humanity. May the stars shine bright on this fantastic journey."

Since John kept talking, I didn't close the quotes after "new world." To remind you that he's still talking in the next paragraph (and I didn't just forget to close the quotes at the end of the first one), I reopen them before, "We don't know."

Five Minutes to Success

Exercise: Practice

Put quotation marks in the right place for these sentences.

I don't know, Jane said. This looks risky to me.

John smiled at the people. We send you off to your new home among the stars.

Ben said, I'm going to read from the famous document that begins with We the people.   (Hint, We the people is a direct quote)

Dialog

Stories run on dialog. When you look at a printed page in a book, there's a good chance you skim over the lengthy blocks of text and scoot right down to the "good part." Your eye wants to do it even if your brain tries to linger on the descriptive paragraph before it. Eyes like white space on a page, and dialog is a great place to do that.

Dialog is, by definition, showing. It's not the author telling us something, it's a character telling another character something. This can be a beautiful thing, and it's also easy to overuse. Many writers fall back on dialog in their worldbuilding, and that leads to the dreaded, "As You Know, Bob" kind of dialog.

The "As You Know, Bob" is when a character reminds another character of something they already know for the sole purpose of sharing that something with the reader. It's fake and stupid and you shouldn't do it. If a character says, "As you know, Bob, we both work for Microsoft, so we understand computers," it's time to rewrite.

Here's a slightly less obvious example.

"I sure love the beach," Jenny said. "Remember our honeymoon in Mexico? We had only been dating a few months back then, because I got pregnant and was determined not to be an unwed mother, so my father forced you to buy me a ring."

As dialog goes, that's not truly horrible, but think about it. Why would Jenny say this to her husband? There's no doubt he remembers why they got married so fast. She isn't reminding him because she thinks he forgot. She's saying it because you, the reader, must need to know they had a shotgun wedding with a baby on the way. It's an obvious "writer thing" that readers see through. If she were having this conversation with someone who didn't know their story, it would be fine. But her husband does, so it's an "As You Know, Bob."

Dialog should always have a purpose. People chatter all day, and I don't want to read every word your character says. Every time someone has a conversation in your novel, ask yourself what the reader is learning from it. This will guide you in how to write it.

Do you want to show that a character is a self-absorbed jerk? A quick scene at the coffee shop where he berates a barista for putting whipped cream on his latte will do that much better than if you just tell me in description that Bob is a self-absorbed jerk. Want to show that Sue has a kind heart? Let's see a gentle conversation with her aging mother about what's going to happen to Mom's cat when she goes into the hospital.

Writing good dialog is a lot harder than good writers make it look. It has to be snappy, to the point, and be true to the character that's saying it. Dialog has to read like actual people talk, only without all the "uh" and "um" and "er" that most folks utter in their speech. Dialog has to be consistent with the time period you're writing in. A Victorian-era medical doctor would not talk like a modern Southern Baptist preacher. Contemporary dialog uses contractions, sentence fragments, and slang.

Here's a bad line of contemporary dialog. In this example, Jenny is a fifteen-year-old girl.

"I am so angry," Jenny said. "I cannot believe you would do such a thing. Were you actually going to try to prevent me from seeing my friend?"

There's nothing technically wrong with that line. It's punctuated correctly, and it's proper grammar. But read it out loud. Try to imagine a high school girl talking like that. Can't do it, can you? Of course not.

So how would I actually write that?

"I'm pissed," Jenny said. "Were you really gonna try that? Keep me from seeing Susie?"

It says the same thing, but it sounds like the character.

Reading dialog aloud (or better still, having someone else read it aloud to you...preferably a human, but there are text-to-speech computer programs that aren't horrible in a pinch) can show you all the places you wrote horrible dialog. If your friend is stumbling over the words, your reader will, too.

And while we're talking about talking, let's spend a few moments on dialects. Dialect is when you phonetically spell something for a character who speaks with an accent. If you're writing about a British Cockney maid, you might be tempted to write her lines as, ""Allo, 'allo, is anybody 'ome? Oh, it's you, guv'nor. Oi've 'alf a mind to bugger off this soddin' job." But with dialects, remember that a little goes a long way. Chances are you had to read that line slowly, and maybe aloud to parse what she was even saying. All the abbreviations and phonetic spellings don't wash through our eyes and into our brains like normal words do. A reader has to work hard to "hear" the language on the page. If I were writing that dialog for real, I'd probably keep "gov'nor" and maybe "soddin'", but I'd spell the other words normally. It's always better to show a dialect through word choice than trying to write out the sound of someone's accent.

Exercise: Practice

Rewrite this dialog in character.

Bob is a forty-year-old truck driver.

"I wish you were not going to leave now," Bob said. "I am sure we could solve our problems if only we could talk about them."

Now Bob is a surfer dude.

"The surf looks amazing today," Bob said. "We ought to leave work early and go catch some waves."

Eavesdropping

So how do real people talk? Generally not the way beginning writers write.

The best way to get an ear for dialog is to listen to people. Coffee shops are great for this. Go get yourself a latte, sit down with your laptop or notebook, and just listen to the people around you. Listen to how they stop and start. How they talk over each other. How one sentence doesn't necessarily flow from another as the speaker's mind jumps around. Listen to old women at the hair salon and young men at a sporting event. Listen to kids talking in the back seat of the car as if their parent wasn't driving. Start hearing the words people choose, and start trying to recreate the conversations on a page.

Remember that in your novel, the dialog must have a purpose. Show me the important moments in your character's story, and let me hear them talking with other characters to advance the plot.

Another consideration is avoiding "talking head syndrome." This occurs when you have two characters in a conversation, and the lines go back and forth with nothing else happening in the scene.

Like this:

"I got a soda from the machine," Todd said.

"Really? I like soda," Sandra replied.

"I didn't get you one because I didn't know what kind you liked."

"I like anything diet."

"Well, I guess I could walk back down and see what they have."

"I'd love that, thanks."

You'll notice two things about that dumb exchange. The first is that I dropped the dialog tags after the first two. That's okay, because I'd established that the only two people talking were Todd and Sandra, and you assume that they take turns speaking. The second thing to notice is that nothing happened. It was super boring because it was nothing but dialog. Just two heads in space yapping on about soft drinks. Dull. No indication of character, nothing to focus on. No way to really picture the scene.

Let's try to spice it up.

"I got a soda from the machine," Todd said.

"Really?" Sandra's eyes fixated on the can in Todd's hand, condensation beading on the side. "I like soda."

Todd's gaze dropped to the floor. "I didn't get you one because I didn't know what kind you liked."

Sandra grinned. "I like anything diet."

Todd glanced back over his shoulder toward the vending area. "Well, I guess I could walk back down and see what they have."

"I'd love that, thanks." Sandra's smile was worth the dollar fifty for a Diet Coke.

Now you'll notice that the dialog here was exactly the same. But this time you got a much clearer picture. Did you feel Sandra's thirst as she looked at the ice-cold can in Todd's hand? Did you feel his embarrassment that he didn't know what to choose, so he didn't bring her anything? And at the end, did you smile along with Sandra, and feel happy for Todd who has a chance to get it right this time? They said the exact same words, but because they weren't just talking heads in space, you could picture the scene. Good dialog should make you feel like you're eavesdropping on the characters, noticing not just what they're saying, but what they're doing, and what they're not saying, which can be just as important.

When I'm writing a dialog scene, here's what I'm thinking about. Does this conversation need to happen (or are we just rehashing things we already knew)? Is this true to the characters? Does this scene advance the plot or reveal something about someone's character? If I cut this scene, would my story lose anything (that goes for all scenes, not just dialog)? Are the characters doing things and not just sitting still and talking (because even if you are just sitting and talking, you're doing stuff. Fidgeting with your pen. Glancing around the room. Wiping your nose on your sleeve. Crossing or uncrossing your legs. Patting the phone in your pocket. All those little actions keep a "sitting in chairs talking" scene from turning into talking heads). And finally, does this sound like people actually talk?

Five Minutes to Success

Exercise: Practice

Enlist two friends to read a scene from your novel out loud. Sit back and listen objectively. Did it sound normal? Stilted? Forced?

Dialog Tags

Try something for me. I want you to smile a sentence. Like this: "I love ice cream," she smiled. Can you do it? Of course not. You can smile while you say it, but you can't smile words. You also can't snort them, hiss them, frown them, or sneer them. Beginning writers love to use dialog tags like this. "I hate you," she sneered. "You're such a pig," he chuckled.

Times change, and writing is subject to trends. At the time I write this, the current trend in fiction is SAID.

That's it. Said. You'll get away with asked, and sometimes replied. Maybe screamed or whispered here and there. But if your writing is full of people laughing out words, or scowling out words, or grumbling words, you're going to be asked to change them.

The same thing goes for unnecessary tags like joked or quipped. If someone is joking, I need to be able to tell that from the spoken line, not the dialog tag.

Like this:

"I like a good murder as much as the next guy," he joked, "but this one is too much for even me."

You don't have to say he joked. I can tell he's joking because nobody would say that and not be joking.

In a case where it's important for your reader to know how someone said something, use a period, not a comma.

Like this:

"That's amazing." Laura laughed. "I'm going to be rich."

Instead of making "laughed" into a dialog tag, (as in, "That's amazing," Laura laughed), I made it the action instead. You can do this with all the facial expressions (glowered, grinned, smirked) that you're tempted to use as dialog tags.

If you read a lot of older fiction, you'll find a lot of "non-said" dialog tags. But like I told you, publishing is trendy. Stick with "said" and you'll be fine.

Now I don't mean you should use it every line. In fact, you should try to use it as little as possible. Remember the dialog from the last chapter? Todd and Sandra and the ice-cold Coke from the vending machine? Go back and read it again. You'll notice that in the better version, I used "said" one time. That's a dialog tag. But all the rest were what I like to call "action tags."

Here's how they work.

Dialog is attributed to the nearest subject in its paragraph. So if you read something like:

"That's crazy talk." Becky tossed the paper away. "Nobody will ever believe it."

You know it's Becky talking here because she's the one with the action tag. She said it, but I don't have to say she said it because I'm showing you what she's doing while she says it. Action tags are always stronger than dialog tags, and it's an easy correction to make to strengthen your own writing.

Like this:

"I'm going home now," Ron said, grabbing his jacket. "See you tomorrow."

It's not bad, but it's a lot cleaner to say:

"I'm going home now." Ron grabbed his jacket. "See you tomorrow."

Eliminate the said, and make your gerund into a verb. Tighter. Stronger. Better.

Oh, and don't think I can't hear your thoughts. "But Wendy," you're thinking. "That's no problem. I can just use said, and then an adverb." Yeah, I know that trick.

Like this:

"You're crazy," Robin said haltingly. "That's impossible."

Do not do this. We talked about adverbs. If you're skipping around through this workbook and didn't read that section, go back and do it right now. Don't put an adverb after your said. Make your dialog do the work of showing me how they're saying it.

Five Minutes to Success

One more thing about tags. If you're having a conversation between two people, the loose rule is that you should have some kind of tag (dialog... she said, or action... she grabbed her coat) about every three or four lines. This eliminates the ping-pong back and forth of just line after line of dialog. You don't have to attribute every single line, because taking turns speaking is assumed.

MASTERING THE CRAFT OF WRITING

Exercise: Practice

Turn these dialog tags into action tags.

Sarah stepped up to the microphone and said, "Hello, everyone."

"I'm going to kill you slowly," Eddie sneered, holding the knife so its edge glinted in the light.

"She doesn't know what she's talking about," Roger said, stuffing his hands into his pockets.

The Dreaded Comma

All punctuation gets abused. Quotation marks are misplaced, exclamation marks are overused, and don't even get me started on semicolons. But if there's one punctuation mark that's done wrong time and time again, it's the comma.

This isn't a grammar handbook. There are already a bunch of those, and you only need one. It's called *The Elements of Style* by Strunk and White, and the answers to just about any grammar question you might have are in there somewhere. I'm not here to be your seventh grade English teacher.

But chances are you're doing commas wrong. I say this because I beta read and edit for a lot of fellow writers, and they all do something wrong here and there. I do it too. The hope is that I go back and find all my mistakes and fix them before they get to you, dear reader, but I make them just like everyone else.

So what are commas for?

The simplest answer is that a comma indicates a pause. If you're reading a sentence aloud, the comma is where you take a breath. It's a lot more complicated than that, but if you keep this idea in mind, you'll eliminate a lot of the most common comma issues I see.

Let's look at some examples.

My cat is sleeping on the floor, dreaming of fat, slow mice.

The first comma is the pause. It's technically setting off the independent clause in the sentence, but that's the kind of grammar talk that makes writers glaze over and skip ahead to a section that isn't about grammar, so who cares? It's the pause. The second one is to separate the two modifiers. The mice are fat and slow. You don't need a comma if you use the "and," but you do need it if you're cramming them together.

The weirdest misuse of this is one I see all the time.

Here it is: The party started at five. But, she wouldn't be attending tonight.

People do that. They'll start a sentence with But (or And, or So, or Although....all of which are technically incorrect if you're an English teacher, but all of which can be used in fiction if it gives your sentences flow). If you start a sentence with But, you don't need a comma. The party started at five. But she wouldn't be attending tonight.

You could fix this grammatically and use the comma correctly: The party started at five, but she wouldn't be attending tonight. Doesn't quite mean the same thing, though, does it? Making it one long thought is very different than making it two independent sentences. Just remember that if you're putting a comma after the first word in your sentence, you might be doing it wrong.

Another place it's easy to screw up commas is in dialog.

Correct: "Hello," John said. "It's nice to meet you."

We use a comma after the "Hello," because we're continuing with the dialog tag. We don't use it after because we're ending the sentence and starting a new one.

Incorrect: "Hello," John held out a hand. "It's nice to meet you."

This is wrong because "John held out a hand" is not a dialog tag. It's an action tag. It should be, "Hello." John held out a hand. "It's nice to meet you." No commas there at all.

Exercise: Think About It

Do commas make you cringe?

Are you strong in grammar or should you spend some time brushing up on your punctuation marks?

Comma Splice

By far the most common error I see with comma use is the comma splice. What's a comma splice? It's the use of a comma to join two independent clauses.

Here's an example: My dog must hear a noise outside, she is barking her head off.

What's wrong there? It's a splice. I've taken two sentences that can stand alone (because they have their own subjects and predicates) and crammed them together with a comma. If I'd included a conjunction (like and, but, or if), it would be all right. My dog must hear a noise outside, because she is barking her head off. Without that "because," it's a splice.

The good news is that they're easy to fix. All you have to do is split them into two sentences. If you don't want to do that, you can add a conjunction between the clauses, or at the beginning.

Here's how:

Splice Sentence: I need to close my window, the rain is coming through the screen.

Conjunction between fix: I need to close my window, because the rain is coming through the screen.

Conjunction before fix: Because I need to close my window, the rain is coming through the screen.

MASTERING THE CRAFT OF WRITING

Using the conjunction in the front turns that independent clause into a dependent clause (which means that "Because I need to close my window" isn't a complete sentence), so it's not a splice to use the comma.

Five Minutes to Success

Exercise: Practice

Fix these comma splices, then look for them in your own writing.

I'm going to the park, I want to play on the swings.

John couldn't believe his luck, he won the lottery.

Coming up with example sentences is hard, they always sound kind of lame.

The Serial Comma

The other place people make a simple comma mistake is in the serial comma, also known as the Oxford comma. If you want to sound intelligent at your next cocktail party, wax eloquent on the lamentable loss of the Oxford comma in modern writing. That's sure to win you friends.

What's the Oxford comma? It's the comma right before the "and" in a list of more than two things.

Here's one now: My laundry was sorted into whites, darks, and delicates.

That comma after "darks"? That's the Oxford.

There are people out there who will tell you it's unnecessary. Technically they're correct. It's not a mistake to leave it out. But it can make for some hilarious misreadings.

Like this: Last week I had lunch with some strippers, my mom, and my grandma.

If you read this sentence you'll likely think it must have been an interesting soup and salad with all those folks at the table. But let's leave out the Oxford comma for a moment.

Last week I had lunch with some strippers, my mom and my grandma.

That makes for a way more interesting sandwich, because I've just told you that my mom and my grandma are both strippers.

Five Minutes to Success

Here's another one: My favorite lunch is salad, soup, and Sprite.

Without the comma: My favorite lunch is salad, soup and Sprite. I suppose I could pour my lemon-lime beverage into the chicken noodle, but that's just gross.

Most professional editors will insist upon the Oxford comma even in places where not using it isn't silly and misleading. It's just a good habit to be in.

Breaking the Rules

We all do it.

All authors break grammar rules. Sentence fragments, ending sentences with prepositions... these things can develop your writing voice and make sure your books sound like you.

But to break the rules correctly, you have to know the rules. You have to understand their place, and know why you're breaking them. It's not enough to just ignore them.

Let's look at a passage.

I gripped the steering wheel, white-knuckled. Rain pelted into the windshield, creating a near-whiteout. When I was deciding to pull over. The blinking yellow of my turn signal distracted me for an instant, and that's the last thing I remember.

What doesn't work there? It's the fragment, "When I was deciding to pull over." That's because it's a dependent clause, and those rarely work as fragments.

Here's a better version: I gripped the steering wheel, white-knuckled. Rain pelted into the windshield. Whiteout. Can't see. Better pull over. The blinking yellow of my turn signal distracted me for an instant, and that's the last thing I remember.

There are three fragments in that one, but it reads a lot better, because the fragments are intentional. They're meant to make you feel unsettled, unsafe. When I'm editing for clients, I'll often make the comment "Unintentional fragment" when it's a problematic one, since I ignore the ones that work and were obviously written for style.

You've already seen how I love starting sentences with But, and So, and And. Technically all incorrect, but when used on purpose, it can create the chatty, informal feeling I'm looking for in this book. I do it in my fiction all the time as well. And it works just fine (see what I did there?).

Rules can all be broken in dialog, because people don't speak in complete sentences. You can use it to help your reader understand a character by the way they talk. Vocabulary and sentence structure tell a lot about a person's education level.

The point is that you could go through any traditionally published novel and use your little red pen to find a lot of "mistakes." But you can be sure that every single one is intentional. Great writers break the rules all the time. What matters is that they knew the rules before they broke them. Make sure you do, too.

Exercise: Think About It

Why do writers talk about breaking the rules so frequently?

What authors do you know who break the rules effectively?

The Beta Reader

You've heard this term before. So what does it mean, and why do you need them?

Beta readers are your first feedback. They're the people who get your manuscript when you think it's ready to be read, and offer ideas on what's working and what isn't. They are precious jewels and you should treat them as such.

There are a lot of don'ts with beta readers.

Don't send them an unedited piece of garbage and expect them to wade through your atrocious comma abuse to see the core of your story. Edit so that what you send them is readable.

Don't expect them to be editors. They're not editors. Editors are editors, and they come way after this section. These are readers who are going to help you determine where your story lags, where your plot holes are, which characters are working, and whether this manuscript is ready to take the next step or not.

Don't ask people who love you to beta read for you. They'll be happy to do it, and it's ok if you want to include them, but you must have a majority of People Who Don't Love You if you're going to get any kind of meaningful feedback at all. Your mom can't possibly be objective about your novel. Neither can your employee whose paycheck depends on telling you how awesome your book is.

Don't give them an unrealistic time constraint. Saying, "Here's my 80,000 word manuscript, and I need detailed feedback in four days," is not going to get you any repeat volunteers.

So here are the Do's.

Do choose people whose opinions you value. If you're part of a writing group, either online or in person, think about the kind of critique they generally offer. Who is the member that always has something insightful to say? That's the person you want.

Do choose readers who enjoy your genre. You want to set them up for success, and asking a hard-core Trekkie to beta read your historical fiction might not be the best idea.

Do choose at least one reader in your target age group. If you're writing for middle-graders, try to get at least one twelve-year-old to read for you.

Do tell them up front what you're hoping to receive in the way of feedback. Do you have a questionnaire you'd like them to fill out for you? If so, it should have questions like, "Did you lose interest in this book, and if so, when?" and "Did you care what happened to the main character?" If you're wanting them to write you a long, detailed discussion, let them know that up front. Some beta readers aren't going to give you more than, "Oh yeah, I read it. Pretty good book." Those are not helpful.

Do choose people who are not beholden to you in any way. They have to be honest in order to be of any value to you. And as much as you tell them, "I want you to be honest," some of your friends/family/coworkers simply can't do that.

How many do you need?

Personally, I send out Beta versions in groups of three to five. More than that and you'll get so many differing opinions that you won't know what to do with them. And you want to keep a few key readers in reserve, because you're going to make changes in the manuscript based on the first round of feedback (yes, you are. If you're not, then one of two Bad Things has happened. Either you chose your readers poorly and they weren't savvy enough to really tell you what the work needs, or you ignored them. Neither of these things will make your book better, and that's why you're doing this). Once you've digested the first round and done your rewrites (which might be as simple as beefing up one of your subplots or characters, and might be as big as cutting the entire first half of your novel), you'll need fresh eyes. Having someone reread your new version is fine, but having a brand-new reader's impression is a lot more valuable.

Where do you find them?

Your writing group is a great place to start. Don't have a writing group? Find one right now. Meetup.com probably has one in your area, but if you're living in the boonies you might have to make due with an online group. There are hundreds of them, and they're not hard to find. Start interacting before you need readers so you're not that annoying jerk who shows up out of nowhere asking for a favor.

If you can't get readers from a writing group, try asking your local librarian. Chances are, she will know some avid readers in your genre who would love to be the first to read your work.

Beta reading time is scary. It's like sending your child off to kindergarten. Will the other kids like him? Will he spill his juice and get laughed at? Will anyone pick him for their dodgeball team? Of course you know that your kid is the best and smartest and will certainly be kindergarten class president by the end of the first day. But you're biased. You made that kid. And you made this book. Waiting around to hear what that first group of readers think about it is terrifying. But if you're planning to publish the work, sooner or later someone who isn't you is going to read it. If it's not the smartest and handsomest kid in school, wouldn't you rather know about that right now, when you can still spiff him up, rather than waiting until he comes home crying because you dressed him funny and nobody would sit by him at snack time?

Exercise: Think about it

Who comes to mind when you think about Beta readers for your current manuscript? How many solid readers could you ask right now?

Part 3
The Art of the Sale

Publishing Options

The Overview

The golden moment has finally arrived.

You wrote it. You edited it. You've taken the feedback of your beta readers and used it to make this manuscript shine.

Now it's time to share it with the world.

What do you do?

Twenty years ago, here's what you did.

You printed out your masterpiece and sent it off to an agent or publisher. And you waited. I don't know how long this used to take, because I wasn't attempting to publish in the days of snail-mail, but however long it took then, it takes just as long now.

What's changed?

Now you have options. They fall into three major categories, and they all have pros and cons we'll discuss in this section.

First, some terms.

Literary Agents are people who work for literary agencies. Their job is to find and sign authors to be their clients, then sell their clients' books to publishers. They are NOT publishers.

Publishers are companies that actually make and distribute books, either physical or e-book. Some are large, with hundreds of employees, and others are one guy working out of his grandma's basement.

Editors work for publishing companies. Acquiring editors are the folks that read manuscripts and decide which ones they love and want to offer contracts to. Large publishers have lots of these people. Tiny ones have just that one basement guy. The other kind of editor is someone who corrects story issues, grammar issues, etc. Some work for publishers and others are freelance (which means you can hire them to spiff up your work before submitting it or publishing it yourself).

Traditional Publishing:

These are the big guys. Penguin Random House. Simon and Schuster. They pay big advances (sometimes) and have huge audiences. They're probably what you think of when you think about finding a publisher. They don't accept submissions directly from authors, so to get near them you need an agent. You'll give up the most control of your work by signing with them, but if you dream about quitting your day job, they're the most likely way to get there (though not the only way).

Small/Independent publishers:

There are hundreds of these in a rotating cast of characters all over the world. They vary in size, expertise, audience reach, and just about every other publishing characteristic you can think of. Some are amazing. Others are useless. All of them accept submissions directly from authors, so you don't need an agent to get a contract. Some will be very interested in your ideas (say, for your cover art), and others not so much. Small publishers are hard to generalize because there's so much variation, but they can be a wonderful in-between for those who don't want to face the brutal slog of finding an agent, but don't want the responsibility of self-publishing.

Self-publishing:

This is when you do it yourself. These days most people use Kindle Direct for e-books and CreateSpace or Ingram Spark for paperbacks. You upload the document and BOOM, it's a book. It's fast, easy, and free. Sort of. It's a way to publish your book today, which is the best and worst thing about it. For those who do their homework, spend their money wisely, take their time, and do it right, it can be tremendous. For those who type "The End" and slap a half-baked unedited hunk of steaming rhino poo up on Amazon and wonder why it doesn't sell, it can be the beginning and the end of a writing career.

When you're training a dog, there's a mantra to live by: Nothing in Life is Free. For dogs, it means that you don't reward behavior you don't want repeated, and your dog has to do something to earn treats and privileges. It works well for dog training, and it's a good thing to remember as you consider your publishing options. None of them are free. Some cost more time, some cost more money, and others will cost you readers if you cheap out on the time and money part. Nothing is free.

The good news is that it's no longer up to someone else whether or not your book gets published. Ultimately, it's your decision, but there are a lot of things to think about before you go crazy and publish something that isn't ready. Read on to learn everything you need to know about your publishing options.

Five Minutes to Success

Exercise: Think About It

What information struck you as important?

What is your personal goal for your writing?

Traditional Publishing

The tried-and-true method of publishing a book is what we'll refer to as "Traditional Publishing." This is when a deal is secured with a large publisher ("Big 5 or one of the smaller but still "bigtime" publishers...these are the ones you've heard of. Simon and Schuster. Hatchette. St. Martin's Press. The big guys whose authors are consistently on the tops of the bestseller lists. This is NOT the same as small independent publishers, which we'll talk about in a bit).

These big publishers don't take submissions from authors. There's only one way in the door with the big guys, and it's through an agent.

So what's an agent?

A literary agent is someone who makes their living selling the rights to manuscripts written by the authors they represent. They are the only way to get a deal with a Big 5 publisher (there's one other way but it's a whole lot less likely, and that's to sell thousands and thousands of copies of your self-published book on your own). They will sell your audiobook rights, your international and translation rights, the rights to the movie, the video game, the T-shirts, and the coffee mugs. An agent is the gatekeeper through which all work must flow.

For this work they take a percentage of your profit, usually around 15%. They do not take money from you.

Let me repeat that.

THEY DO NOT TAKE MONEY FROM YOU.

If you are approached by an "agent" who asks YOU to pay THEM, then they're not actually an agent. They're scam artists and you should run very far, very fast. In a real agent/client relationship (where you, the author, are the client), money flows TO the author, not from. You don't pay them a penny until they sell your book. Then the publisher pays them and they cut you a check after taking their percentage.

How do you get one?

There are a lot of ways to get an agent's attention.

The traditional way is the query. This is a cover letter that resembles the back-cover blurb you'd see on a paperback. The tease about your story that grabs their attention and makes them want to read your work. We'll talk more about queries in another chapter, but the simple answer is, you send a query (possibly with your opening chapters included, depending on what the agent wants), and you wait.

The waiting hasn't changed.

Sometimes you'll hear back right away.

Sometimes not. And sometimes you'll never hear back from them at all.

Your query will go into the "slush pile," which is all the unsolicited queries the agent has received. She will peruse them and choose some that interest her, requesting more pages if she likes what she sees. There may be some back and forth suggestions (called a "Revise and Resubmit" where they ask you to make changes, then send it back for them to re-read...this is not mandatory, but most authors are happy to revise based on agent feedback when it's looking promising).

If they love your manuscript, they'll make an offer of representation. You'll sign a contract that gives them exclusive rights to sell your work.

There are other ways to get an agent's attention besides the unsolicited query.

If you're on Twitter (and you ARE on Twitter, aren't you?), there are "Pitch Parties" held regularly. More on those later.

You can meet agents at writing conferences. Now I don't mean that you should try to corner one in the ladies' room. They frown on that, particularly if you're a guy. But most larger writing conferences feature "Pitch Sessions" where you pay an extra fee (usually) and get five or ten minutes to sit down with an agent and pitch your book. It's a great chance to talk with them face to face and share your excitement about the project. If they like what they hear, they'll invite you to send them either a partial or full manuscript.

Do what they say.

It's tempting to think, "Oh, she asked for the first fifty pages, but I'm sure she'll love it. I'll save time and just send her the whole thing now."

Do not do this.

It's partially a test. There are secret rules in the agent game, and seeing if you can follow directions is one of them. Send exactly what they ask for. No more, no less. Show them you were listening, because if you're not listening now, you're not going to listen when they ask for revisions before they submit your manuscript (and they will. Never forget that writing is re-writing, and now you get professional advice on how to do it).

Some agents offer boot camps and lectures on sites like Writers' Digest. You can sign up for their courses and sometimes get a critique included. Occasionally they'll like your work enough to ask for more, and the conversation can begin there. These are also a great learning tool because so often when you're querying you'll get no feedback at all. You send out the query and hear nothing, or if you're lucky, a form rejection. They don't have time to respond to every query, so if you're getting a lot of rejections, you won't know why. This is a great way to find out.

The other way to get an agent is to be very lucky, and know someone who has an agent and who likes your work enough to recommend you to their agent. This is a tricky subject, and a great reason to be part of a writers' group. Networking rules in publishing, just like everywhere else. If you have a critique partner who is agented, you can ask them if their agent represents the kind of work you're writing, and if they would recommend you to her. But you have to be prepared for them to say NO, and to not be offended by this. How many people do you know who have written novels? Chances are it's a lot. If you're the lucky one with the agent, they'll all want to jump on board. You won't be able to say YES to all of them, and you might decide it's your personal policy to say NO to all of them to avoid hurt feelings in your writing group. So it's fine to ask, but if they refuse, then accept that gracefully and move on.

The odds are not in your favor. Most agents receive between 4-500 queries each week. From these, they accept 5-10 new clients a year. Do the math. It's not pretty.

There are just so many writers out there. It's easier than ever to churn out 80,000 words, and agents are deluged with hopefuls. You have to get very lucky with a superior manuscript that's in great editorial shape that lands on the right desk of the right agent at the right time.

Here's a quick personal story to illustrate this. I wrote four manuscripts before I got an agent.

The first three were speculative fiction. Two fantasies and a science fiction. They were good. Two of them eventually got published. But none of them got me an agent, despite me sending over 60 queries for each one.

I was halfway through my fourth fantasy novel (which remains unfinished to this day). There was an online critique event where writers all over the world would submit their queries and opening paragraphs on a huge bulletin board system. Everyone could read and comment on everyone else's work, so you could get a lot of feedback fast.

Mine went up and got some nice reviews. And I started reading everyone else's.

Sci-fi. Fantasy. Fantasy Fantasy Sci-fi Fantasy Sci-fi Paranormal Fantasy Fantasy Sci-Fi.

They were almost all speculative fiction. One after another, and they were all good.

Hundreds of them. Just as good as mine.

And I thought, *No wonder I'm not getting any attention.*

So I changed gears and wrote a murder mystery.

I sent out five queries. This resulted in two phone conversations with agents.

Within a month of starting to query, I was represented.

Now, a lot of things changed here. This was my fourth completed manuscript, so I'd learned a few things. My older stuff was good, but this mystery was better.

And I got lucky. She was looking for a good mystery writer at the very moment my manuscript came across her desk. If she'd signed someone else the day before, I'd have gotten a rejection from her instead of an offer. It would have had nothing to do with the quality of my work, just the timing.

I tell you this story not to dissuade you from writing speculative fiction, or trying to get an agent with an epic fantasy. It can be done. But it's always worth remembering that sometimes there are factors you don't know that play in to this decision.

However you do it, if you want a Big 5 Publishing deal, you need an agent. It might take several years, but it's possible.

From here on in, it's up to them.

They'll write a pitch letter and start submitting to the big publishers. And you will wait.

There's nothing more you can do at that point except trust your agent. It can take a while. Or forever. You might end up writing another manuscript if the first one doesn't sell. But you'll do it with the advice of a literary professional, and the value of that can't be overstated.

When they receive an offer on your manuscript, they'll contact you and you'll be on your way.

Remember that Nothing in Life is Free.

Five Minutes to Success

Exercise: Think About It

Why would you do all this work?

Why do you want an agent and a big publishing deal?

What is Your BIG Takeaway From this?

Pros and Cons of Traditional Publishing and Why it is Important

Pros:

Payday. The only publishers that still offer advances are the big guys. A few of the larger indies might, but mostly they only pay royalties. You'll most likely get more royalties from a large publisher, though, because you're more likely to sell more books. And if you don't have an agent, who's going to sell the movie rights? The translation rights? The audiobook rights? Maybe no one, and those are all ways that a single manuscript can keep putting dollars in your pocket.

Advice. Are you writing a novel right now? Of course you are. When it's done, will you want someone to read it and tell you what they think? Of course you will. Do you wish that someone could be an industry professional with years of experience and a deep knowledge of publishing trends and publisher wish lists? Of course you do. Once you have an agent, you'll have all those things. I still have beta readers and I still self-edit like crazy. My agent gets my very best, most polished work. Then we start rewrites because she knows what is most likely to sell and what my manuscript needs to stand out. When you start querying and getting form rejections, you'll be willing to sell a kidney for just one agent to tell you why they rejected you. What didn't work?

What can you do to fix it? Once you get an agent, you have that forever.

Cost. It takes money to make a decent book. Someone has to pay for things like editing (because no matter how good you are at grammar, you will miss things in your own work. And story editing is a lot more than just making sure you've used "their" and "they're" correctly), cover art (nearly as important as editing, because if you have a crappy cover, no one's going to read your words anyway), formatting (ever seen a poorly formatted e-book? Just one long paragraph for the whole thing? It happens), and proofreading. If you self-publish, you're paying (one way or another...more on that later). If you have a publisher, all those upfront costs are paid by them, not you.

Publicity. No matter how you publish, a lot of this still falls to the author. The days of national book tours are over unless your last name is King. But big publishers have built-in audiences. They know how to get ARCs (Advance Review Copies) into the right hands for the professional reviews that will get your book into Barnes and Noble, libraries, and major book awards. They're your ticket to A-level blurbs ("This book scared the pants off me."--Stephen King), national book festivals, and if all goes well, to the bestsellers lists. All those things can be acquired by the dedicated, professional self-publisher, but only after years of work.

Distribution. If you want your books on the shelf of the national chain bookstores, there's one way to do it, and that's traditional publishing. They don't carry self-pubs, and although they can order and sell books from the smaller publishers, they only do it when someone requests a specific title. Same with libraries. They decide what to carry based on professional reviews. So if your dream is to see your hardcover novel at Wal-Mart, start writing your query now.

Legitimacy. This is a tough one. When I say, "legitimacy," I don't mean quality. There are a lot of amazing self-published books out there. Some are better than a lot of what the Big 5 are churning out. But most of them aren't. Most of them (and I do mean most of them...there's a new title on Amazon every four minutes) are poorly-edited, poorly-formatted, poorly-proofread drafts that should have had months of professional work before seeing the light of day. And everybody who's ever bought a 99 cent e-book and read three pages before going, "Wow, this is a giant steaming pile of rhino poo," knows that. So when you finally get published, the first thing people are going to ask you is, "Did you self-publish?" If you answer yes, they'll nod knowingly. "Ah," they'll think. "Good old YourNameHere wrote a book and published it him/herself. Isn't that nice." And if you answer no, I'm with Hatchette, they'll say, "Holy potatoes, you mean the Harry Potter people?"

Now, this isn't about impressing your friends. But if you know that John's book was self-published, and Jane's is with Hatchette, whose do you KNOW will be edited, formatted, and proofread? Whose book do you trust that even if you hate the subject matter, at least it will be of guaranteed minimum standard of quality? That's what I mean by legitimacy.

This might not be remotely important to you. If it isn't, you're braver than me. When I started this roller coaster, I made a decision. I thought my first novel was pretty darned good. But I decided that if not one agent or publisher agreed, I wouldn't publish it. Out of hundreds of agents and hundreds more acquisitions editors for small presses, if not one of those people thought my book was good enough for them to put their names on it, then did I really want to put it out there with my name on it? I didn't. I needed the validation of an industry professional to say, "This is good enough," before I was brave enough to put it out for the world. You might be a lot braver than that. But it's something to think about before you hit "Publish" on Kindle Direct.

Exercise: ***Think About It***

Do you agree or disagree with Wendy's decision to not self-publish if she couldn't find a publisher?

Organize the pros in order of importance to you. Are any of them negotiable or not an issue?

Cons:

Traditional publishing is slow. I'm talking geologically slow. I am typing this draft on the last day of 2016. My agent is submitting a manuscript right now. If it sells, it might be published in 2018, and more likely 2019, because big publishers filled all their 2017 slots two years ago. And most people take at least a year, and usually a lot longer, to get that agent in the first place. Your mileage may vary, but agents and traditional publishing are not for the impatient.

Control. You'll give up the most control with a big publisher. They aren't interested in your ideas for cover design. You'll likely have no say in that whatsoever. They'll write your back cover blurb. They'll have the final say on editorial disagreements. They might suggest big changes, and you'll either say yes, or you won't have a Big 5 publishing deal anymore. If you're the type who is able to trust that they know more about selling books than you do, you'll be fine with that. Decide before you sign that contract.

Control. I just said that, but this time I mean that you can't control when you'll get an agent, and if you do, when she'll get you a publishing deal. You'll write the best manuscript you can, but ultimately it's not up to you. If they want you, they'll sign you. But if they already have a stable full of epic fantasy writers or alt-historical writers or mermaid erotica writers, then no matter how good yours is, they won't be interested. Same with the publishers they submit to. If you're not selling what they're looking for at the exact moment they're looking, you're out. So control what you can, but know that some of it is in the hands of fate.

Exercise: Think About It

Do you have the right temperament to slog down this long, slow road?

Can you exercise patience, endure the inevitable rejection, and give up control in hopes of seeing your books on the shelf at Barnes and Noble?

Self-publishing

Maybe traditional publishing isn't for you.

Maybe you don't have the patience to wait years before seeing your book in print. Or maybe you write in a niche genre that isn't likely to have the kind of mainstream appeal that agents are looking for. Remember that they don't earn a penny for working on your book. They only earn a percentage of what that book earns in sales. So if your target audience is small enough that they aren't likely to make a decent amount for the hours they spend editing and selling it, they're not going to take you on as a client. The math just doesn't work.

Maybe you're a control freak who can't stand the thought of anyone else's ideas contributing to your work.

Or maybe you have tried to get an agent to notice you but haven't been among the lucky few who got the call.

Any of those are valid reasons to forego the agent search.

In the past, you'd have two options. Give up or vanity publish.

Give up still exists, and so does vanity publishing. There are publishers out there who will publish your book no matter how good or bad it is. You give them money, and they publish your book. Vanity publishing is a paid service, and though true self-publishing has eroded their client core, they still exist. But the key here is that you give them money.

True self-publishing is free* (huge asterisk here...because remember when I said nothing in life is free? I meant it).

Here's a scenario. Let's say I've been keeping my grocery lists for the past forty-five years. Maybe I've augmented it with some other people's grocery lists, because I wasn't actually writing my own the day I was born. The point is, lots of grocery lists. I can compile these into a "book." And I can publish that "book." And you, hapless reader, will have no idea when you go to that Amazon site and see "Milk and Bread: A Grocery Story" by D.W. Vogel whether this is a well-written novel full of intrigue at the checkout line or... a bunch of grocery lists.

It's an extreme example, because you could probably tell from the opening pages that I hadn't actually written a novel. But when you peruse the millions (yes, millions...over seventeen million titles at last estimation) titles on Amazon right this minute, you have no way of knowing if my self-published novel is great or terrible. All you can see is that it costs ninety-nine cents.

This is the danger of self-publishing, and what's given it a bad name.

Make no mistake. There are some excellent self-published novels out there. Also great non-fiction, memoir...you name it. But the percentage of wheat to chaff is so much lower. The good ones are a much smaller fraction among self-published novels because absolutely anyone can publish anything and call it a novel. It takes about five minutes and a computer. That's all anyone needs to be a published author these days.

A few have hit it big. There are a few names you'll see with regularity when you look up "self-published author success." Some of those authors are formerly traditionally published, agented authors who decided to leave their contracts and strike out on their own. They are skilled craftsmen who learned the old-fashioned way how to write a compelling novel, but either got tired of giving up control to their publishers, or hoped they'd earn more on their own by not sharing the price of each book with a publisher and an agent. They developed a fan base through traditional publishing, then took those fans with them when they left. Whatever your personal feelings about this, it has worked for some of the self-published successes you've heard of.

Others were just plain lucky. Right book, right time.

The fact is that the average novel sells less than two hundred copies.

Let that sink in for a minute.

Less than two hundred. So if these are paperbacks you've printed and sold yourself, you probably earned between two and six dollars for each one. E-books probably got you a dollar each.

If we math that out, you've earned about six hundred dollars, depending on how many e-books versus paperbacks you sold.

Maybe time to delete that nasty resignation letter you've penned to your boss.

I recognize that all this is meaningless to you. I can hear you right through time and space, as I sit at my computer and type these words. "But, Wendy," you're saying. "That's all well and good for normal authors. They're terrible. I'm great. My book is going to sell millions. I'm not that 'average' writer, so your statistics don't apply to me. Now where's that yacht catalog again?"

To that I say, "Good for you." I love that kind of optimism. And for you, my friend, I hope it's true. I hope that someone who reads this book and uses its advice to craft a superior novel gets out there and sells a bazillion copies and retires to an island in the Caribbean. If that's you, I hope you remember your dear friend Wendy who helped you so much. But if you're relying on luck to get you there, I'd suggest holding off on the down payment for that beach villa.

Successful self-publishing takes work. A ton of work. Because everything's up to you.

You need an editor, and probably more than one.

"But Wendy," you say, "I'm great at grammar." Uh huh. So am I. But I still miss things. And so do you. So does every editor in the world, and every proofreader. It's why publishers employ a whole fleet of them and the occasional typo still sneaks through.

"But Wendy," you say, "Grammar doesn't matter anymore. I have a computer program that fixes it, and really, nobody cares anyway if the story is good enough."

That sound you just heard? That was me slamming my head into the wall. Again. I've heard this all before. And I don't know why I think you'll listen to me, but I am duty-bound to say it. Grammar matters. Formatting matters. Ever read a whole novel with no paragraph breaks? Of course not. You wouldn't get past the third page. But they're out there because some enthusiastic author hit "publish" and didn't care about proper formatting.

And more importantly, grammar and formatting matter right now. With this first novel. Because guess what? If I buy your debut for ninety-nine cents on Amazon, and I see that you have grammar errors on the first page, I'm done. Not just with this book. With you. Forever. I will never buy another of your books, even if the next one is titled, *I Swear I Paid a Professional Editor This Time!* You are dead to me because you betrayed my trust. And I'm far from the only one. It's so easy to destroy your writing career before it ever begins.

Pay an editor. Preferably pay at least two. You can find reasonably priced freelance editors online. Do your homework. Read books they've edited to make sure they know more about grammar than you do (because anyone can slap up a website and sell their editing services. There are no governing bodies, so buyer beware). You'll pay at least $500 for a short-ish novel, and could pay up to a few thousand for a longer work or a more established professional. Suddenly that six hundred dollar paycheck doesn't sound like much.

Pay a cover designer. When you look at a page on Amazon or Barnes and Noble, what do you see? Tiny thumbnails of book covers. What catches your eye and makes you read the description? To put it another way, how much is it worth to you for other people to notice your book cover out of the seventeen million other covers they can page through? If you don't have a professional cover, it will be assumed that you don't have a professional book. This was true even before the advent of e-readers. Years ago I was in a local bookstore strolling through the sci-fi/fantasy section. A young employee started chatting with me, trying to find out what sort of book I was looking for. He handed me a copy of Matthew Stover's *Heroes Die*. He said, "Here's the book you should read. It's the best book with the worst cover you'll ever see." He was right. The book is fantastic. And the cover is simply dreadful. I would never have picked it up and read the back jacket, and I'd have missed out on a tremendous read. Don't let this happen to you. You might not be lucky enough to have a bookstore employee on your side.

Pay someone to format for you, or be darned sure you know how to do it yourself. It's always a good idea when self-publishing to download a copy for yourself on whatever e-reader you're publishing on. Make sure it looks right before your launch.

I bet you're seeing dollar signs flashing in front of your eyes right now, aren't you? You're thinking about how much all this will cost. But it's the cost of doing it right, and if you don't, it will show. Choose carefully before you put something out there with your name on the cover.

Exercise: Think About It

Can you afford to pay professionals to make sure your work is pro quality before you self-publish it? Can you afford not to?

How to Self-publish

So how do you do it?

There are lots of self-publishing options.

As usual, Amazon is the 800 lb gorilla in the room. Their Kindle Direct publishing service walks you through all the steps of uploading your manuscript, formatting for Kindle, setting your price and categories, and uploading your bio and cover photo. They make it as easy as they can to do this fast. This is a wonderful and terrible thing. By the time I finish writing this section, you could be a published author. You could take your finished manuscript, whatever shape it's in, slap a stock image and font on the cover, and foist it upon an unsuspecting world.

It might be brilliant.

Or it might be unfinished. I don't mean incomplete, I mean unfinished...not truly the finished, professional product that's going to make people who don't know you want to pick up your book.

What other options are there?

Barnes and Noble has their own e-book service called Nook Press. Or you can hire an outside company like BookBaby to help you with all the formatting and distribution. This is not the same as a vanity press, because they aren't publishing your work. They're getting paid for the drudgery of helping you do it yourself.

You can also create a high-quality paperback through Amazon's CreateSpace or the independent Ingram Spark. These are Print-On-Demand services where a buyer chooses your book and pays for it, then it's printed and mailed to them (within a couple of days). This keeps you from ending up with a garage full of cardboard boxes containing the saddest books of all...the unsold ones.

Consider your distribution before you choose. If you only want to distribute through Amazon, you can publish exclusively through their services. This unlocks a lot of free help through their website, but limits you to Amazon-only sales (which is where most of your sales will probably come from anyway). If you want your book available on all platforms, you can still publish through Amazon and Kindle, but not exclusively.

It isn't difficult to navigate through these choices and create your finished product. There's no one to tell you you can't, you shouldn't, you're not ready. The rest of this book was designed to help you GET ready, and prepare your manuscript for whatever publication route ends up working for you. If you go the traditional route, you'll have gatekeepers along the way...agents and editors who won't let you publish something that's not ready (in their opinions). When you traditionally publish, you'll have the confidence of an agent's and publisher's name on your work, their seals of approval that what you wrote is strong enough for them to want to claim it.

If you go it alone, only you can decide when you've rewritten enough, edited enough, designed enough, and formatted enough to hit "Publish." This is the beauty and the curse of self-publishing.

Exercise: Think About It

Are you computer-savvy enough to handle self-publishing on your own, or should you hire a company to help you navigate?

Are you brave enough to push the button?

What resources do you have available to use if you self-publish?

Self-publishing Pros and Cons

Pros:

Fast. You can be published tonight. No agent has to choose your manuscript from the hundreds of queries they receive each week. No editor has to fight for your work in their staff meetings. The timing is all up to you.

Control. Everything is up to you. No one else will suggest changes to your characters, your story arc, your theme, or your writing style. No one will choose a cover for your book, whether you love it or hate it. You choose the launch date, you choose the publicity angle. Sink or swim, it's your pool party.

Rights. You keep them. All of them. If you decide to change the manuscript, you can pull it down and change it. If you want to record an audiobook, you can hire voice talent and record it. The video games, the T-shirts, the movie rights and the action figures...it's all up to you. And while the chance of any studio finding your book and wanting the buy the movie rights are, well, one out of over seventeen million, it's still your chance.

Royalties. They're all yours. Whether you sell ten books or ten million, you don't have to share the proceeds with anyone (except Uncle Sam, but that's another book).

Cons:

Fast. Nothing is making you wait, so why not do it tonight? Millions of hopefuls have said those words. They've sold about twenty copies of their unedited, poorly-formatted steaming hunks of literary rhino poo, mostly to their families who are too nice to mention the smell. And that's all they're going to sell, because they launched a lump of coal when they should have waited for a diamond.

Control. Everything is up to you. The only help you'll get is help you're paying for, and the well-meaning advice of family and friends who may have no idea what they're talking about.

Royalties. A recent New York Times article found that out of hundreds of thousands of self-published authors, only forty of them were "making a living" (described as selling more than a million ebooks in the past five years). So while it's great that you get to keep all the royalties yourself, if you're not selling books, then you're keeping all of basically nothing.

Publicity. Like everything else in self-publishing, publicity and marketing are up to you. Remember those seventeen million titles on Amazon? There's a new one approximately every four minutes. One of them could be yours, and that's great. But how are your readers going to find you? Amazon isn't going to promote you until you have enough verified reviews to get into their secret algorithms. And even then, it's not much. We'll talk about what you can do to promote your book elsewhere, but if you go it alone, you will have to do everything yourself. And Tweeting "Buy My Book" twelve times a day is a great way to lose all your Twitter followers and sell nothing at all.

Legitimacy. Again, I don't mean quality. There are good and bad self-published books, and good and bad traditionally published books. But here's what happens. Let's say you decide to self-pub. You're at a party and meeting new folks. You tell them you're an author and your first book has just been published (because, remember, you're the only one doing your publicity, so you're telling EVERYONE). They smile and say, "Oh, did you self-publish it?" Your eyes drop. "Yes." Their smile becomes knowing and they suddenly have a pressing need to use the bathroom, or refresh their drink, or grab a couple more of those stuffed dates from the buffet. Let's contrast that to what's going to happen if you're traditionally published. "Oh, did you self-publish?" the partygoer says. "Nope. I'm with Hatchette." They choke on their kalamata olive. After you perform the Heimlich, you wipe the dribble from their chin. They say, "Hatchette? Like Harry Potter?" You smile. Yes. Like Harry Potter.

How did that last bit make you feel? It's what I mean about legitimacy. The old stigma of vanity publishing has persisted into the modern world of self-publishing, largely because it's so fast and easy and there are so many truly horrible self-published e-books out there. Yours is going to be lumped in with them. It doesn't mean yours is bad, good, or otherwise. But it's the company you'll be compared to. This may not be important to you, and I remain in awe of the confidence shown by self-published authors who know their work is good and are happy to tell anyone about it.

Exercise: **Think About It**

Which of these pros appeals to you most?

Which of the cons worries you?

Do you need the approval of a literary professional before you are confident in sharing your manuscript with the world?

Small Publishers

What if neither of the above options appeals to you? You want help...professional editors and cover designers. You want a network of people who have a stake in making sure your book is a success. You don't want to wait years to see your book in print, but you don't want to launch a steaming turd into the world with your name on the cover.

There's another option.

Independent/Small Publishers span that gap.

They're real publishing companies ranging in size and expertise from one person with a computer to huge companies with salaried employees. They're the hardest group to talk about because there is so much variation. Some of them are worse than doing it yourself because you'll be getting bad advice and locking up your rights with a company that has no idea what they're doing. Others are tremendously successful, with strong networks and publicity rivaling the Big 5. And everywhere in between.

Indies tend to be genre-driven, focusing on one niche market in order to keep their readers coming back. There are sci-fi indies, fantasy indies, romance, horror, historical...any genre you can think of, there's probably an independent publisher who's looking for it.

You don't need an agent. They accept queries directly from authors. This doesn't mean they're easier to get accepted by, because there are still hundreds of hopefuls every week for very few publishing spots. But there are a lot of indies, and most of them are dedicated to finding new voices. They're looking for you right now.

Indies are much quicker to respond and faster to publish. Instead of years from acceptance to publication, it's usually less than six months. There is no cost to the author (remember, if you have to pay them, they're not an indie. They're a vanity publisher and you should run away).

Some of them are e-book only, and others offer paperbacks. Of the latter, some do traditional print runs and others work Print-On-Demand, only printing an individual book once it's sold. Either way is fine. I've had both, and the quality difference is indistinguishable.

When your manuscript is accepted by an independent publisher, they'll send you a contract. Because you won't have an agent to look it over for you, it's wise to hire an attorney familiar with contract law to make sure you're not signing away rights you shouldn't. The publisher will acquire the rights for a certain period of time, and for a certain format (such as: all English language versions, or all English e-book versions). They may retain other rights as well (such as the right to sell movie rights and merchandise). Your percentage as the author will be spelled out for each right they are contracting to acquire. There should be a clause about what happens if the book doesn't sell or goes out of print, and what happens to your rights if the publisher goes out of business (which is all too common). It will likely also say that the publisher retains final say in edits and proofreading issues. Many authors get scared at this moment, thinking the publisher is going to swoop in and make a bunch of changes. They are, but you'll be part of those changes, and you'll have plenty of input. They will not write for you. Every word will still be yours. But they may have ideas you never considered, and they may find issues you never noticed. The book will always be yours, but it's no longer yours alone. This is usually a very good thing.

Once the contract is signed, you'll be assigned an editor. There are a lot of ways to accomplish editing. Shared documents that you can both make comments on are common, as is just emailing versions back and forth with comments and version numbers. The publisher will tell you how they do it.

For *Horizon Alpha* I had three editors. First was a developmental editor, who helped me reorganize some chapters, and suggested places where my ideas just weren't working for her. She made her case and I made the changes (which turned out to be absolutely the right call for this series). We sent versions back and forth until we were both satisfied. Then they sent me to a copy editor. She went line by line with me, making sure each individual word was the right choice in the sentence. She wasn't commenting on the story, but on the actual nuts and bolts of writing. When that was finished, the manuscript went on to proofreading to make sure none of us missed anything.

While all that was going on, I was working with the publicity department. Future House, the independent publisher for *Horizon Alpha*, has a number of bestselling novels because they know how to help readers find their books. We worked on my email list, my review list, author blurbs, and launch month/week/day activities. We continue to work on publicity opportunities like personal appearances and interviews. The publisher makes money when *Horizon Alpha* sells, so they care just as much as I do that the book is a success.

The art department created my cover. I had some input (which, for *Horizon Alpha*, amounted to, "There should be a dinosaur on it," because beyond that I trusted their expertise).

With a small publisher, you'll get royalty checks directly from them based on the agreed-upon rate per book (in your contract).

Your Mileage May Vary.

As stated, independent publishers range from amazing to useless. I got lucky this time and found a great one. My first published novel wasn't so lucky. It was published by a different indie which was mostly the brainchild of a single well-intentioned person who had very limited experience in the fiction world. My editor (singular) was good, and I loved my cover, but she knew little about publicity and I knew even less. That publisher no longer exists, and that novel went out of print. The rights were returned to me and I have self-published it to keep it in the world, but no other publisher is interested in a manuscript that didn't sell the first time, even if that had nothing to do with the work itself.

This kind of thing happens all the time with independent publishers. So if this is the route you choose, do your homework. Before you submit (or at least before you sign), buy several of the indie's other books (e-book and paperback if they offer it).

Look at the covers.

Read the books.

Are they clean and error-free?

Are they well-edited in story, and sentence by sentence?

If it were your book, would you be happy with the quality?

If the answer is no to any of those questions, keep looking. It's much worse to sign with a bad publisher than not to sign at all.

Exercise: Think About It

Does the idea of an independent publisher appeal to you?

Do you like this compromise of speed, control, and assistance?

Small Publisher Pros and Cons

Pros:

Help. You'll get professional assistance with editing, proofreading, formatting, and cover design. The quality of this assistance could be great or terrible. Do your homework.

Speed. Your book can be published this year instead of two or three years from now.

Legitimacy. Someone out there likes your manuscript well enough to put their own names on the cover. It's validation for your work and legitimacy for anyone that asks who your publisher is (because, let's face it, with a few exceptions most people have no idea who publishes anything. So even if it's a small company, it's a company that chose you for their stable).

Publicity. If you choose an experienced publisher, they should be able to guide you in your publicity efforts, and will have some of their own. Most of the actual work (social media, getting reviews, making appearances) will still fall on your shoulders, but that's true even with the Big 5. They want you to succeed, but you NEED you to succeed. You're one of their authors, but you have only yourself.

Cons:

Control. You'll give up some control of the work. Your editors and art department may have their own ideas that you'll have to find a way to be okay with.

Royalties. The publisher will pay you on their schedule. Mine pays twice a year. So if you're counting on a monthly income, you had better excel at budgeting. And you won't know for sure how much the check will be, because you don't have direct access to your sales figures.

Rights. They aren't yours anymore. If you decide you don't like your publisher, or you want to make changes to the manuscript, that's too bad. It's theirs now, for whatever period of time was in your contract. It's a legal business document and they own whatever rights you signed to give them.

Quality. There are as many bad ones as good ones. Don't get so caught up in the idea of having a publisher that you make a poor decision.

Five Minutes to Success

Exercise: Think About It

Which of these Pros appeals to you most?

Which of the Cons is most frightening? Can you live with that fear?

Cover Art

Go look for a book on Amazon. Even if you never shop there and always buy your books from a local bookstore, just go open a browser on your computer or phone and browse the virtual shelves. What do you see?

The first thing you'll notice is that there are millions to choose from no matter what genre you're looking at. Each book cover will be an inch high at most, depending on what kind of monitor or phone you're using. You might get the first few words of the back jacket copy, but mostly you'll be presented with a row of tiny book covers.

How do you choose one? Let your eyes roam down the page. What's grabbing your attention?

It might be a cool-looking font. It might be the name of an author you know, or maybe a catchy title. Maybe it's a picture that makes you want to click on the book. Whichever one catches your eye, you'll most likely click on it and read the blurb.

That's the book cover's job.

For most books, it's the only part that anyone will ever see, the lonely little rectangle amid all its competitors. If the cover doesn't jump off the page and into someone's brain, it's going to get scrolled over. You have to do this right.

If you have a traditional publisher, you won't likely get much say in your cover. That surprises a lot of first time authors, but the publishing house has an art department who does one thing all day long, and that's book covers. They're better at it than you are. Trust them (because you don't have any other choice). If you're with a smaller indie publisher you might get some input, or at least be asked for suggestions. When the first *Horizon Alpha* novel came out, my only request was that it had to have a dinosaur on the front. Beyond that I knew my publisher would do a much better job than I ever could, and I was thrilled to pieces with the cover they came up with.

If you're going to self-publish, you'll either have to do it yourself or hire someone to do it for you. This won't be cheap, but besides editing, it's the absolute best thing to spend your money on when you're trying to sell a book.

What makes a great cover? If I had a certain answer, I wouldn't be writing this book, I'd be in marketing making millions of dollars. No one knows a guaranteed formula. But here's what you have to have.

A readable font. If your book title isn't immediately legible, you're done before you start no matter how cool your picture is (with the possible exception of romance, which relies a lot more heavily on the muscle-bound hottie on the front).

MASTERING THE CRAFT OF WRITING

It doesn't matter if your book title is top, bottom, or middle of the page, but it needs to be big enough to read at Amazon's thumbnail size. The same goes for your name. Even if no one knows it now, the hope is that someday your name will sell books on its own. Don't make me have to hunt for it. And if you can use the font to tell me something about the book (think Emma Donoghue's bestseller *Room*), that's like getting two for one.

Then there's the colors and the image. The *Twilight* series sold a bazillion copies with a black background and hands holding an apple. *Hunger Games* had the mockingjay pin symbol. Other successful books use models or landscapes, or drawings that evoke a feeling. There is no magic formula. There are a lot more "don'ts" than "do's."

Don't make the cover so busy that you can't see what's going on at a glance.

Don't use a stock photo you found online.

Don't use a copyrighted photo that isn't yours (really don't do that one).

Don't pick an image that has nothing to do with your book just because you think it looks cool or will make people pick it up.

This is one area where paying a professional cover artist can earn back what you put out. If you're not a graphic designer with loads of marketing experience, do yourself a favor and find someone who is, and give them money to make sure your book cover has a chance of being picked from that tiny Amazon page.

Mastering the Craft of Writing

Exercise: Think About It

What kinds of book covers tend to draw your eyes?

Are you more likely to read the jacket copy based on a cool cover or interesting blurb?

Five Minutes to Success

Submission Overview

If you've decided that self-publishing isn't right for you or for your current work, it's time to think about the submission process. Whether you're submitting to agents hoping for a Big Five deal, or to independent publishers directly, you'll need a submission packet. A lot of writers have said that putting this together is harder than actually writing the book. It's certainly true that distilling your 80,000 word novel into a two-paragraph query letter and a one-page synopsis can be daunting. But it's the only way to get anyone else interested in your project, so it's time to hold your nose and jump in.

For the sake of simplicity, I will say "agent" in this section when I refer to the person you're querying. If you're not looking for an agent, but hoping to get in with an indie publisher, that person will be the acquiring editor, but the process is exactly the same.

The most important advice I can give you is this: FOLLOW DIRECTIONS.

Yes, I put that in all caps. Because it's that important.

Every agent you query and every publisher you submit to will have submission requirements. You'll find them helpfully listed on their websites. Which means that as you're making your list of who you think would be a good fit, you'll have to begin by going to each website and finding out what they want. This will be up to three things, with a few small variations.

The Query. The Synopsis. The Opening Chapters.

We'll talk about queries and synopses in detail in the next sections. And all I can say about the opening chapters is that I hope you've followed all the advice in the "editing" sections, and gotten good beta reader feedback to help you make them perfect, because if there are errors in the opening pages, none of the rest of this will matter.

Remember those awful statistics? Here are some more. I'm a client of PS Literary and my agent tweeted her agency's stats from 2016. They received 14,863 queries in that year. That's about 285 queries each week. From which they usually choose no more than about ten new clients. I'm not telling this to scare you into not trying, but I am telling you because they're looking for a reason to delete yours. This is not because they're jerks who want you to fail. It's just because they are so overwhelmed with hopefuls that they have to start eliminating somewhere, and if you prove right out of the gate that you didn't bother reading the submission requirements, or didn't bother to follow them, why would they continue looking at your submission? If they can cut down the number of opening chapters they have to read by, say, half right off the bat because you didn't follow the rules, think of the time they'll save. No query letter? Delete. Included attachments instead of pasting the text right into the email?

Delete. No synopsis? Delete. If they keep this up, they might actually get a lunch break today. So don't let them.

"But Wendy," you say. "My stuff is so good that..." Nope. Doesn't matter. Because if you don't follow the rules, they're not going to read it. Doesn't matter if you're the next J.K. Rowling, your boy wizard will never find the magic stone because they won't even read the first page if you don't follow the guidelines. You won't get a chance to convince them that you're too good to follow the rules, because you're already deleted. It sounds harsh, but it's the reality of modern publishing.

A few basic thoughts on this process.

It's awful.

No matter how good you are, you're going to get rejections. You have to be ready for that. And I know you're thinking, "Sure, everybody else gets a lot of rejections. But my stuff is so good that..." Nope. You're going to get rejections. If you've bought this book and are reading about how to do this, it's because you don't have the intimate contacts in the agenting and publishing world to sidestep this grueling process. Absolutely everybody gets rejections. They don't mean you're bad, or your manuscript is bad. They just mean there's so much other good stuff out there that today was not your day. Prepare for this emotionally however you can, because it's going to be a lot worse than you think.

How can you improve your odds?

We already talked about the first rule, which is: follow directions. Send them exactly what they ask for. No more, no less. If they ask for the opening three chapters, don't send them chapters 10-13 (because that's when it really gets good....to which I reply, "Then cut chapters 1-9 and start there.). Don't send them the entire manuscript (thinking, "Well, it's so good they'll want to just keep reading, so I'll save them the trouble of asking." Nope. Remember, this is a secret rule game, and if you break the "following directions" rule, you're out).

Don't send attachments unless specifically asked. Most agents won't open anything with an attachment because it might be a virus. Copy and paste everything into the body of the email. It goes: Query Letter Body (space) Opening Chapters (space) Synopsis. All in one long email. It looks weird, but it's safe for them to open and read.

Be polite, and use proper etiquette. Dear Jane is not appropriate. Dear Ms. AgentLastNameSpelledCorrectly is. You don't know her, so don't pretend you're friends. This is a business letter, so be professional. Always remember that everything you do as it pertains to your writing (query letters, Twitter posts,

Facebook/Instagram posts) should reflect who you are as a writing professional.

Never respond to rejection. You may be very tempted to write back on a form rejection with something nasty like, "How can you reject me when you haven't even read the whole thing?" Don't do this. Don't be a jerk, either in email or online rantings. Agenting is a small world. They talk. Don't make them talk about you. Part of this process is convincing an agent or publisher that you're going to be a joy to work with (because they'll be spending a ton of their time on your manuscript before they ever earn a penny from it, just like you have). No manuscript is good enough to have to work with a jerk.

Some of them will include an expected time frame for replies. They might say, "If you haven't heard from us in three months, please email to be sure we received your submission." If they don't have a statement like this, you'll have to assume that no news is bad news. Some agencies and publishers respond with a form rejection to every query, but others don't. Often the answer you get is no answer at all. I recognize the irony of how unprofessional that seems, and that I've just spent a whole page telling you how you have to be so professional in these dealings, but we don't get to make the rules here. We're just playing the game.

Decide if you're querying agents or small publishers. Don't do both at once. If you do get an agent, the last thing she'll want to hear is, "Great, let's start submitting. Oh, and here's a list of thirty publishers who have already rejected this book." Not the way you want to start your agent/client relationship.

In the next sections we'll look in more detail at the query and synopsis, and at other pitching options.

Five Minutes to Success

Exercise: Think About It

Are you ready to persevere in the face of rejection?

Can you follow someone else's rules to find success?

The Query Letter

Entire books have been written on the subject of query letter writing. Many great websites exist to help writers find the elusive alchemical formula that will get an agent's attention and make her want to read your chapters.

I'm a veterinarian by trade. One of the things I've learned in twenty years of private practice is that when there are a lot of different ways to treat a disease, it's because none of them work 100% of the time. Query letters are like that. Nobody really knows the secrets. What might entice one agent will certainly drive another screaming off a cliff. There isn't one right answer. Here's what I do know.

The query letter is the business letter you write to introduce yourself and your work to the agent or publisher you're hoping will be interested in your novel. It has three basic parts (the order of which is your call because agents are on record as preferring them in every possible order, so you can't hope to please them all. Just make sure all the parts are in there.): the personalization and book information, the query body, and the biographical information.

It begins, as business letters do, with a salutation. Every literary agency's website has bio information on their agents and what they're looking for. Pick the one you think will be the best fit and address it to him or her. Dear Ms. Smith. NOT: Dear

Agents of XYZ Literary. NOT: Dear Agent. Absolutely not: To Whom It May Concern.

I usually put the personalization and book information first. Personalization is why you chose this specific agent to query. Your honest answer might be, "Because your name was next on the list of a hundred agents I made up when I started this six months ago...Dear Agent 73." Do not say this. Instead, find something you think they'll connect with. They all have bios on their websites. Most of them have Twitter accounts you can follow, and many have published interviews you will find when you search their names online. You might say, "Because you represent AuthorName, I think you'll connect with the uplifting theme of my novel." Or, "I read on Twitter that you are looking for women's fiction with non-traditional protagonists. I think you'll love CharacterName's feisty humor." Honest to Todd, I once personalized a query with "I read in your Writer's Digest interview that you love Biscoff cookies. I often choose to fly Delta just to get a packet, so I thought we'd be a good match." I didn't get a request from this agent, but I did get a nice reply that wasn't a form letter. At least I know she actually read my submission. The point is, what you write doesn't matter so much as that they know you didn't just throw darts at a list of agent names. You picked them from the agency for a reason.

While we're on that subject, here's another tidbit. Even if they don't specifically say it on the website (many do), you can only query one agent per agency with the same manuscript. And don't think you can sneak it by them by just changing the title. They work together. And even if they work from home, they talk to each other all the time. Choose wisely, because if one rejects you, that manuscript is done for that agency. You can query again with a new manuscript.

In that opening paragraph along with the personalization, you'll need to include the data on your book. This includes genre, age group, title, and word count (rounded to the nearest thousand). So you would say, "I'm thrilled to share NOVELTITLE (in all caps), a young adult mystery complete at 72,000 words."

Oh, you noticed I said "complete," did you? Right. Very important. If your novel isn't complete, put this book down and go finish it. You can't start querying fiction until it's done (and edited, and corrected, and beta read, and revised and revised and edited).

It's all right to say, "a fantasy novel with series potential." It's not all right to say, "the first novel in a planned series of ten," even if it is. This first novel has to be self-contained. No cliffhangers. It must be complete and stand alone even if it's setting the stage for a trilogy or one of those detective series that lasts as long as the alphabet. You are querying one book. One. That's it. Telling them it's the first of a planned twelve, or telling them how much money they're going to make, or telling them how sorry they'll be if you let them slip past is an instant ticket to Deletesville.

Now we move on to the good stuff.

The body of the query is like the back jacket on a paperback. It's the story tease that makes an agent reach for her mouse to scroll down and read your opening chapters. It does not include the end. The best ones are catchy, specific, and written in the voice used in the actual book (which does NOT mean writing the query from a character's point of view...that's an Insta-Delete for probably every agent in the world...I mean that the query and the chapters sound like they were written by the same person.). It should be one or two paragraphs long, and must include your main character and antagonist. It's written in third person present tense, as in: Simon Pacificus, the most powerful wizard in all Atlantis, has a secret; he's afraid of the water.

A good rule of thumb to remember is that you want to share the character, the conflict, and the stakes. So: Who is the main character? What does she want? Why can't she get it/what's standing in her way (that's the conflict)? What happens if she doesn't get it (that's the stakes)?

Don't be vague. Agent's don't want to read about "an evil threat that lurks in the forest." They want to read about the vengeful tree-spirit that's found a way to escape her tree. Or the ancient bug-monster who's just awakened from his thousand-year hibernation and is hungry for human blood. Whatever it is, it's what makes your story unique. Don't make them guess. They won't bother. If you're stuck, go to your local bookstore and pick up a bunch of paperbacks. Read the back jackets on each one and really think about which ones grab you and make you want to buy the book. What about that particular story compels you to open your wallet? Find that in your own book and make it sing.

The last part of your query letter is the biographical information. This is where you list other things you've published, including short stories, magazine articles, or professional publications. You might not have any, and that's fine. Just say, "This is my first novel." Don't lie, and don't embellish. Your high school newspaper doesn't count. The basic rule is that if they couldn't go online right now and find the publication, then it's too small to mention. And it really is okay if you don't have anything to list here. You might be tempted to write about your profession here, and that is all right, but only if it pertains to the story you've written. For example, if you've written a police procedural, then it's great to include in the bio that you've been a Kansas State Trooper for twenty-five years. But if you've written a high fantasy about elves, nobody cares if you're also Cleveland's number one Toyota salesman for 2014. If it's relevant, include it. If not, then know that your writing is strong enough to speak for itself.

Close your query with "Thank you for your time." Don't say anything egotistical like, "I'm sure you'll enjoy working with me," or, "I look forward to making millions of dollars with you." Don't tell them when you expect a reply. Include your contact information, and move on to the next part of the submission packet.

Mastering the Craft of Writing

Exercise: Think About It

What is the most interesting thing about your novel and how can you distill it into one or two paragraphs that will catch an agent's attention?

Who is your main character, what is the conflict, and what are the stakes?

The Opening Chapters

Most agents will ask for the opening bit of your manuscript along with the query letter and synopsis. Their website will tell you how much, but the first three chapters, or the first one chapter, or the first 500 words are common requests.

This is your chance.

The query letter is important because from that the agent will decide if she has any interest in a book like this. If she does, she'll give you a try and read the opening chapters you've helpfully pasted below the query in the email.

Your whole manuscript has to be in perfect shape. But these first chapters...they have to shine. If they're remotely interested in your premise from the query, most agents will give you one page. One single page, by the end of which they'll have decided whether to read another or hit the dreaded Delete button. It sounds unfair, but remember that you're one of about fifty queries they have to get through that day before they can even begin working on all the other things agents actually get paid to do, like sell clients' books. So you have to grab them fast.

There are a lot of don'ts, and none are absolute. A few writers have sneaked through with cliché openings, but most of the time these things will get the Insta-Delete:

Opening with a dream sequence (because it feels like a bait-and-switch...we open with your character riding a unicorn through a pink forest...then the alarm clock buzzes and she wakes up in her boring bedroom, ready to start a boring day. If I thought this was going to be a pink unicorn story, I'm already gone). This leads directly to...

Opening with your main character hitting the alarm clock (or throwing it across the room). Cliché, cliché, cliché.

Opening with an infodump. Common in sci-fi and fantasy, this is where you spend pages and pages explaining the geopolitical history of your world, its magic system, its government...and it's an Insta-Delete for most agents. All that worldbuilding information is important, but it's not going to draw a reader in. Start with someone doing something. It's that simple.

Opening with a line of dialog. This occasionally works, but if you open with a line like, "Oh my gosh, he's dead!" you'll think you're starting at a crucial, tense moment and I'll instantly be drawn into the story. But I don't know who's talking. I don't know who's dead. I don't know why he's dead, or how he relates to the person I don't know who's talking, and as a result, I don't care. I know you're going to explain it, maybe even in the next sentence, but you want your opening sentence and paragraph to place your reader right into your story, and you can't do that by floating words in space. You have to give me something to picture in my mind before somebody starts talking.

If the agent is interested at the end of the first page, she'll likely read to the end of the first chapter. By that point, something has to have happened. She needs a reason to turn the page. You have to have either posed some question to which she MUST know the answer, or relayed some mystery she wants solved. It's not enough to have a strong world and an interesting character. She needs something concrete, some unanswered question that she can't go another minute without pursuing. It doesn't have to be overt. It could be a seemingly normal situation with just one little incongruity...one little thing that makes her say, "Wait a minute, what's really happening here? All is not as it seems." If you can do that, she'll read on.

I shouldn't have to say this, but I have to say this.

There cannot be grammatical errors in your opening chapters.

Here's why.

If all goes well and the agent reading your chapters decides to offer representation (the fancy way of saying, "I want to be your agent, let me sell your stuff."), she's going to be pitching it to acquiring editors at the big publishing houses. Before that happens, she'll guide you through some revisions to make it the best version it can possibly be. She will read your manuscript several times through over the course of a couple of months or longer before it's ready to send out. What she is NOT going to do is edit for you. If she's reading a manuscript and seeing comma splices, dangling modifiers, wrong punctuation, etc., what she's thinking is, "Boy, howdy. This thing would take me weeks of work to get into shape for an editor to read it. I don't have that kind of time." Because, really, why should she? If you haven't taken the time to edit your manuscript, why would she? At the moment she's looking at your chapters, she has forty-nine others sitting on her computer waiting to be considered. If the choice is between one that's in great shape and only needs some story massaging, and one that needs a full copy edit, why would she ever choose the one that's a mess? "But Wendy," you say, "My story is so good she won't care. She'll be happy to fix my commas and semicolons because...elves. And vampires. And fairies." Nope. Not going to happen. Because she won't get past the first page if it's full of errors. She'll never get to the elves and vampires and fairies. You'll be deleted before you ever began, and because you'll only get a form letter rejection, you'll never even know why.

***Exercise:* Think About It**

Are your opening chapters ready to go?

By the end of Chapter One, has there been a question asked that must be answered?

Has there been something compelling enough to force a page turn?

What will the reader know by the end of Chapter One that makes your novel unique?

Synopsis

The word strikes fear into the hearts of writers everywhere. The dreaded synopsis. Difficult to write, uninteresting to read, it's a necessary evil of the submission process.

It exists for one reason: to prove you know how to plot.

Every portion of your submission package shows the agent something specific. The query letter shows you're serious enough to look them up, find their submission requirements, write the letter, and that there's something special about your novel to interest them. The opening chapters show them if you're a decent writer. The synopsis shows that you can put together a whole novel and have it make sense.

There are a lot of people out there who can write an amazing short story. They have strong voices that grab readers and pull them in. But writing a short story and plotting a whole novel are two very different things, and before an agent invests six to eight hours reading your entire manuscript they want to be sure you know what you're doing. Do you have a beginning, middle, and end? Do your conflicts get resolved in a satisfying manner? Do your characters grow and change? Are there loose ends or, heaven help us, a cliffhanger? These are the questions your synopsis must answer.

Here's how you break it down.

Five Minutes to Success

A synopsis is written in present tense, third person. It follows the main plot of the novel all the way through to the end (spoilers included). That's pretty much it. The first time you introduce a character, their name goes in ALL CAPS. After that, write the name normally.

Here's an example from Horizon Alpha: Predators of Eden.

Fifteen-year-old CALEB WILDE leaves the safety of the electric fences surrounding his colony on the distant planet Tau Ceti e. Along with his squadron of young soldiers, he flies out on the last working shuttle to retrieve a power core that will keep the fences charged and the last of humanity safe from the dinosaurs that hunt the jungles.

It's not meant to be beautiful writing. You just tell the story, beginning to end. Most agents want a one-page synopsis, single spaced. It's a lot harder than it sounds.

Every time I've had to do it, I've turned to Susan Dennard for help.

She wrote a brilliant post on Publishing Crawl at PublishingCrawlhttp://www.publishingcrawl.com/2012/04/17/how-to-write-a-1-page-synopsis/ and I use it every time. It's a fill-in-the-blanks template that helps you break down the most important parts of your story to put in your synopsis. Without that resource this chapter would be a lot longer, but honestly she's done a better job than I ever could at laying out the basics of how you write a synopsis that isn't horrible (because they're all bad, but as long as they're not horrible, you're all right. Remember, this is just judging the plot. There can't be grammar mistakes, but it's not where they're judging your writing. Much.).

Not every agent asks for one up front. You might decide you're just going to query the ones that don't, but some of them are sneaky and if they like your query letter, they'll email you back and ask for your synopsis. Don't let that be a pants-changing moment. Have one ready.

So just check out that website, chill the frosty beverage of your choice, sit down, and write the thing.

Five Minutes to Success

Exercise : Think About It

What will be the hardest part of distilling the plot of your novel into one page?

Which subplots can you ignore?

How can you show your main character's growth through the basic telling of your plot?

Revise and Resubmit

Sometimes in the querying and submission process you'll get what's called an R and R. This stands for Revise and Resubmit, and it's a very good thing.

When an agent or editor rejects your manuscript, but gives you an R and R, here's what it means. They can't accept your book as it stands right now, but there's something about it that they love. The R and R will say something like, "While we cannot accept your manuscript at this time, we would be open to reading a revised version." They will proceed to suggest the revisions they want to see.

This is not a guarantee that they'll accept it if you make those changes. You might make them, resubmit them, and they still don't love it. Chances are your manuscript will be stronger for the revisions, so you've at least got that.

The changes might not work for you. If they don't, just move on. You aren't required to resubmit.

But an R and R means you're close. It means that whatever isn't working for that agent or editor is something they think you can fix, and they're willing to tell you exactly what they want you to change. Sometimes this will be very specific (cut the filtering, cut the expletives, give us more sensory depth in specific scenes), and other times more general (The ending is too bleak. We need some sign of hope for the main character). Consider their suggestions.

Your first instinct might be to shout, "No way, it's perfect as is and you're stupid for wanting me to change anything." It's all right. You can shout that. Then go back and re-read their suggestions. Sleep on it, and read them a third time. Really think about what they're saying. Decide if you can try the revisions they want to see.

If you can't, you might honestly consider self-publishing. An R and R is every querier's dream...the agent is telling them exactly what's wrong with their manuscript, and what they have to change to get accepted. After fifty form rejections that leave you scratching your head and going, "Yeah, but WHY? What don't you like? Why is it always NO?" to get an agent's personal feedback is huge. I had two R and Rs on the manuscript that finally landed me my agent, and each one made it stronger. It's also good practice for when the manuscript is accepted by a publishing house. If you can't make changes to get in, they know you won't be receptive to the edits they'll require before publication. It comes back to the control thing. If you can't imagine taking anyone else's advice on your manuscript, you won't handle a professional edit from a publisher well, and you're probably not a good fit for traditional publishing.

If you read the revision suggestions and agree that they might help your work, dive in and make some changes. Know that an

R and R isn't for tiny tweaks. If a manuscript only needs tiny tweaks, they won't bother with an R and R, they'll just accept it. Edits will follow. An R and R means there's something big enough wrong (in their opinion) that they cannot accept the manuscript as is. The changes have to be made. I suspect in some cases it's also a test to see how willing you will be to follow advice and make changes, because that's a way of life for traditionally published authors. Do not fail the test.

Don't rush. They don't want it back in a day or a week. Not even a month. An agent doesn't expect an R and R for at least six weeks, and if it takes you six months, they're fine with that. No one is ever in a hurry in traditional publishing (except the author). They want you to take your time and make it right. If you rush through and make a couple of little tweaks, you'll blow your chance. A final rejection after an R and R is truly a final rejection.

Take all the time you need. Let the work sit while you mull over their suggestions. Figure out what made them want the revisions, and how you can make them work for you. Dive into the revised version with the same enthusiasm you had when you wrote it the first time.

This is a great opportunity. Someone likes your book. They like it almost enough to offer to represent you, or to offer you a publishing contract.

FIVE MINUTES TO SUCCESS

Seize the day and make it happen.

Exercise: ***Think About It***

What's your plan?

Pick a writing buddy and bounce ideas off another author. Who do you trust? How honest are they about your writing?

Other Pitching Options

What we've just discussed is the traditional way to get your work in front of an agent or publisher's face. When you hear about "the slush pile," that's what is meant. Before computers and email, the slush pile was literally a pile of papers, unsolicited manuscripts that would arrive on agents' and editors' doorsteps. They would pile them up in a corner and page through them when they had extra time and wanted to find new clients. Now it's just a folder on their desktop, but the name is the same.

It's not the only way.

Well, it kind of is the only way, but there are other ways to move your manuscript from the bottom of the slush pile to the top.

We talked earlier about Twitter. While it's mostly used by authors as a way to connect with fans (and potential new fans), it has one other fun function in a writer's life.

Pitch Parties.

About once a month, there will be a pitch party on Twitter. This is a day when a specific hashtag will be searched by participating agents and indie publishing editors looking for interesting pitches.

Here's how it works.

A given party will have a specific date and hashtag. This might be #sfpit or #adpit,   (for sci-fi and adult manuscripts, respectively), for example. If you have a sci-fi manuscript, you would pitch on SFPit day. On Twitter you get 140 characters, and your pitch has to fit in one tweet that includes the pitch hashtag and also a hashtag for your age group or genre if appropriate. For AdPit, any genre is welcome, so you might write #adpit #wf for women's fiction (you do this because the agents will search only for what they represent. Thousands of pitches will be flying by all day.). Then you have the rest of the 140 characters to pitch your story. Basically, one long sentence, or a sentence and a half.

It's a lot harder than you think.

You can search those hashtags right now and see what other writers have pitched. Read through some of them and see which ones look interesting to you. What did those writers say that made you look twice at their pitch among all the others?

Here is mine from when I was pitching: 15yo Caleb must return with the power core through a dinosaur-infested jungle. If he's late, his family is what's for dinner.

You learned a lot from those few words, didn't you? You know the hero is fifteen, so it's a kid book. You know he's a boy. You know there are dinosaurs. You know the conflict (getting through a jungle) and the stakes (dinosaur dinner). If you're an agent who's looking to fill out your ranks with a kidlit sci-fi dinosaur adventure, you've just found one.

Five Minutes to Success

If an agent or editor favorites your pitch, it's an invitation to query them. Click on their profile and look through their tweets. Somewhere in their recent feed there will be instructions, something like,"If I favorite your pitch, please send query, synopsis, and first three chapters to..." and contact info. While this might seem no different than the normal unsolicited query, it's actually a great leg up. Now you can open your query with, "Dear Ms. Smith. I was thrilled that you favorited my pitch during yesterday's Twitter event." Now they know that at least one sentence of your manuscript interested them. You've jumped to the top of the pile.

Another way to get noticed is face to face pitching at writing conferences. Most major cities host at least one conference during the year. When you look at the offerings, you'll see if agents are participating. If they are, you'll have the chance (usually for an extra fee) to sign up for a pitch session. This gives you five or ten minutes (it will be specified) to sit down across the table from the agent and pitch your book.

What will you say? If you have ten minutes, you should plan a three-minute speech. You don't want to spend the whole time on a pre-rehearsed monologue that's going to sound like bad community theater because you're a nervous wreck (and you will be a nervous wreck. This is an AGENT. A real live AGENT. Sitting across the table from you, sipping coffee and waiting for you to stop fumbling around and forgetting your name and for the love of Todd will you just SAY SOMETHING?). It's okay to bring a few notes. She knows you're petrified. It's your first time, but not hers. Just tell her about your story. Tell her what makes it special. Be real, be humble, be honest. Then shut up. She'll ask you questions and hopefully you'll have a conversation. At the end of your time she'll either tell you that it doesn't sound like the right fit for her, or she'll invite you to submit to her. I did this twice, and both times was invited to send my full manuscript. Some agents will ask you to send a partial, and some might just ask for a formal query letter (which you will open with, "It was so nice to talk with you at ABC Conference," so they remember who you are and where they met you).

The more wily of you might be thinking, "That's a great idea. Why go to conferences? Just send my manuscript to an agent and claim we met at a conference and she requested the full. They see so many people, she'll never remember." Yes, she will. And you'll be blacklisted forever. Do not do this.

Also do not corner the agent in the ladies' room, or the breakfast buffet, or the parking lot after the event. Pay for your ten minutes, and use them wisely. Stuffing a thumb drive under the door to her hotel room will make her remember you forever, just not the way you want. And agents talk.

If you're not comfortable with the face to face pitch but still want some feedback, check out Writer's Digest. They offer webinars and boot camps all year long that feature agents representing all genres. They're not free, but many of them include the opportunity to get honest critique from the agent on your material, usually the query letter or first few pages, depending on what the webinar is about. Lots of agents find new clients this way, and even if they don't fall in love with your work, you'll get some strong feedback on what's working and what isn't.

MASTERING THE CRAFT OF WRITING

Exercise: Think About It

Which of these alternative pitching opportunities appeals to you?

Do you have the time and money to attend a writing conference in person or a paid webinar online?

Agents and Publishers--Where to Find Them

Even if you're the least computer-savvy writer in the world, you're going to need online access. Most agencies and publishers don't accept snail mail queries anymore, so you'll be spending a lot of time on the internet. It's where the agents are.

There are two great sites I recommend: AgentQuery and QueryTracker. If you prefer a physical book to page through, Writer's Digest publishes a yearly *Guide to Literary Agents*, which is a great resource. But always double check each agent's website before submitting to make sure nothing has changed since the book was published. Their wishlists are constantly evolving as they find new clients and develop new interests.

And speaking of wishlists... do you know about #MSWL? You do now. It stands for Manuscript Wish List, and it represents both a Twitter hashtag, and a couple of websites dedicated to the cause. This is a great way to narrow down your list of agents (because if you've already checked out AgentQuery you've found out that there are literally hundreds of agents out there. This is a good thing because there are also thousands and thousands of hopefuls sending queries, but makes it hard to decide who would be a good fit for your manuscript).

Search #MSWL on Twitter (see why I told you it was important?) and see what the professionals are hungering for. You might see one that's hoping to find a historical fantasy set in ancient Rome. Or a western romance with a spunky female lead. Or a children's book that makes her laugh out loud. Read the posts and see who's out there looking for what you have to offer. Move them to the top of your list (and remember to use this in the personalization on your query!).

Build a list. I know what you're thinking. "But Wendy," you say, "I won't really need a list. My book is so awesome that I only have to pick which agent I want. Once she sees it, I'll be done and on my way to the Caribbean." Maybe you're right. Probably not. In fact, almost certainly not. This isn't because you're bad, it's just math. So build your list. I use Evernote, but any word processing program or spreadsheet will do.

You'll need to keep track of the agent you're querying and the agency name (because remember that a no from one is a no from the whole agency, so don't annoy anyone else there. They keep notes), the date you queried and what you sent (including a version number because if you're not getting positive response from your initial query you're going to revise it. You can't re-query an agent who already rejected it, but you can at least keep track of what people are responding to), the date their website says to expect a response (if any), and the response. Leave space for notes like, "personalized rejection, invited querying other works," or "Full request January 5, reject March 6." These notes will help you if you decide to query another work in the future.

Send out five to ten queries at a time, and wait at least a few weeks before sending out more. The temptation will be to splatter your query all over the internet, sending it to all 87 agents on your list at the same time. But despite all your work, your query might suck. If you send it to ten or twenty agents and get no requests or personal rejections, just form rejections, you might want to revise it before you send it to anyone else. Don't put all your eggs in one huge basket just in case your basket turns out to be made out of wet kleenex.

Exercise: ***Think About It***

How will you narrow down the list of agents you want to query?

Do you have the patience to wait for responses that sometimes never come?

Make a list of agents to research.

Rejection

This is a hard chapter to write.

Jeri and I are writing this book because we've met so many writers over the years that keep asking the same questions. How do I write a good novel? How do I get published? How do I find a publisher? The sad fact is that sometimes the answer is, "You don't."

Everyone gets rejections. It's the nature of the business. Even if you don't attempt the traditional publishing route and just do it yourself online, you're still going to get bad reviews, if you're lucky enough to get any reviews at all. Harry Potter got rejections. And no matter how many times I tell you this, and how prepared you think you are for when the NOs come rolling in, you're going to be devastated. You've spent months, years on this manuscript. Agents will reject it without reading a single word. Worse, agents will reject it after reading every word. It happens to all of us and it's something you have to consider.

Sometimes all the NOs are just a prelude to the YES. Sometimes the rejections spur you to take a deeper look at your manuscript and make the changes that will make it good enough to sell. After fifty or a hundred rejections you might decide to hire a professional editor or join a writing group to get some honest feedback (because if you've shown it to your mom and your friends and they all said it's perfect but you've gotten a hundred form rejections, or fifty form rejections and fifty long, deafening silences, you need to consider getting some more objective critiques). You might decide to set this work aside and start something else.

For most people, the process takes years. There aren't any official statistics about how many people get an agent or publisher with their first completed manuscript, but when you start reading author blogs and meeting other writers, you'll find that a lot of people have a manuscript in the hard drive equivalent of a dusty bottom drawer. Sometimes more than one. This is soul-crushing but it happens more often than it doesn't.

It's hard to realize your work isn't good enough. We all expected our first effort to be perfect.

Why do we do this? If we were taking up any other avocation...golf or bowling, or learning to speak Spanish, we would expect to spend months or years being terrible at it before we got good. If you go to Paint Nite, where you drink wine and follow a teacher in the front of the room, trying to replicate his painting on your canvas, you don't honestly think your "Silhouette of Tree in the Sunset" is going to hang on a museum wall. You know it's going to look like it was painted by a monkey on a trampoline, and that's okay. You're not a trained painter.

But with writing? Nope. That first novel, that first story...they're flawless. Every single word a glittering gem.

Let's think about art for a minute. Real art. The kind that gets painted on the ceilings of churches in Vatican City.

Do you think this was his first one? Do you really think that this masterpiece, the Sistine Chapel, was the first time Michelangelo picked up a brush?

Of course not. We've never seen his first attempt with a paintbrush. He must have painted countless versions of "Silhouette of Tree in the Sunset" over and over, covering up each one until they got less and less suck, and eventually started to be decent.

He practiced. He learned his craft.

But not us. No, not us writers.

It's because we're readers, and good writers make it look so easy. All we see on the bookstore shelves are the final, rewritten, edited versions of their work. We read these stories, these novels and we say, "Well, of course I can do that."

And we can. Just not very well at first.

But we read, so we think we can write. Which is akin to saying, "Well, I've been eating food my whole life. So I'm sure I'm a master chef. Just hand me that knife. Now which is the sharp side?"

Or, "I've always lived in a house. I work in a building. I know what walls and floors and stuff are all about. So hand me those blueprints and a hammer, because I will certainly be a master builder this first time I grab a nail."

Ridiculous, of course, but it's what we do as writers.

And it's why the rejection hits so hard.

The best advice I can give you is to start writing something else. Right now. While you're in the middle of the query trenches, checking your email every 42 seconds to see if anyone responded to your last round of attempts. You're going to get rejections, so you need to have something else cooking already or you'll find that the old cliché of writers as a bunch of depressed loners pounding away at their computers in the dark with a lapful of cats is based on reality. You won't necessarily get more cats, but depression is a very real thing and it's going to nibble away at your happiness bite by bite.

Start something else. It doesn't have to be another novel. It absolutely 100% should NOT be the sequel to the novel you're querying (because what if Book One doesn't sell? "But Wendy..." Nope. It might not sell. No matter how good it is. It might. Not. Sell. Now you've wasted a lot of time on a Book Two that no one is ever going to read. Or maybe Book One will sell, but your agent will suggest some changes and your editor will suggest more, and suddenly that character from Book One who was a handsome Spanish bullfighter is now a feisty German barista. And also a girl. Which makes the plot of Book Two, where the dashing toreador meets a fair maiden over the carcass of a bull he's just killed, kind of weird because now they're both women and one of them is making coffee. This kind of thing happens. So don't waste time on Book Two until somebody gives you money for Book One).

But you should be writing another book. Or some short stories. Something unrelated to Book One entirely.

You'll need them for your mental health.

Another novel is great because you'll be able to tell yourself, "Well, I got another rejection today. But that's okay. Because even if this first manuscript goes nowhere, I'm working on something even better, something they're sure to love." And it's more likely to be true, because you'll be using the skills you learned on the first novel on this new endeavor. It will be better. It can't not be.

Short stories are great because you can bang them out in a lot less time than another novel, and you can try to sell them on their own. Lots of publishers do regular anthologies that are open to all submissions. You can get a short story published a lot faster than a novel, and that's good for two reasons. One is that now you have something to put in the bio section of your novel's query, an actual publication you can reference. The other is that it's a yes.

The road to the big YES is paved with little YESes. Mostly NOs, but also some YESes. And you'll need them so you don't lose hope. Short story accepted into an anthology? Yes. Partial request from an agent? Yes. Favorite on a Twitter Pitch Day? Yes. These small affirmations that you do have promise, you are a good writer, will keep you going down the long, dark hallway of no.

Exercise: Think About It

Can you persevere in the face of rejection?

Are you prepared for a multi-year course of action?

Do you have another idea you can be working on while you query this novel?

Don't Cop Out

So now that I've crushed your dreams of finding an agent and a publisher, you might be thinking, "Well, I'll try for an agent. And if I don't find one, I'll try all the independent publishers. And if none of them want it, I can just self-publish it."

You're right. You can do that.

But do you really want to?

If you want to self-publish because you feel it's the right choice for you and your work, then do it. Do it slowly, do it professionally, and do it right. Don't do it as a fallback.

It's not a safety net for unpublishable work, though a lot of people use it that way. Like we talked in the chapter on self-publishing, you can publish anything. You can do it tonight. By the time I finish typing this section you can be a published author. And that's great. And terrible.

You can ruin your chances that way forever, because chances are this isn't the only book you're going to write. If this book isn't ready for the world to read it, but you put it out there anyway because you're tired of rejection and you just want to be done with it, already, it's out there. Even if you decide it was a mistake and take it down, the internet is forever. Someone will have a copy. And if you didn't find an agent because you didn't edit well, or your characters were flat, or your plot had canyons, or it was 200,000 words, that's not going away. And when you decide to try again with another work, it's still going to be there, haunting you.

If it's still published and you're querying another book looking for an agent or publisher, you can bet they'll find it unless it's in a pen name. And if you don't try for an agent with another book, your potential audience might already have crossed you off their list of "authors who can write a decent book that's worth $.99 on Amazon" because your first one wasn't ready but they bought it anyway and now they will never trust you again.

Self-publishing has been a boon to writers in niche genres, those odd works that a traditional publisher won't touch because they know the audience isn't big enough to earn back the money they'll spend producing it. It's also wonderful for memoirs of non-famous people, those folks who want to preserve their family histories or personal stories for their children and grandchildren (because let's face it, most people's stories just aren't interesting enough for anyone not related to them to want to read it. If Something Amazing hasn't happened in your life, I'm probably talking about you). It's great for odd-length works like novellas that aren't going to find their way onto bookstore shelves unless your last name is King. It's great for those with established platforms, like popular bloggers, who have a ready-made audience. And it's great for anyone who wants to be able to say they're a published author without spending years of heartache perfecting their craft.

But it's a terrible fallback option.

If you want an agent and a publisher, get one. If not with this book, with the next. Or the next. Keep working, keep writing, keep learning, because it's not over unless you quit.

Exercise: Think About It

Was that your plan all along?

Are you rethinking it now?

What's your new plan?

Twitter

You need Twitter. If you don't have a Twitter account, go open one right now. I'll wait.

Okay, are we back? Good.

Now what's so important about Twitter?

Let's start with what it is. Twitter is a social media option where each post is limited to 140 characters. Tweets are meant to be quick snippets of thought, broadcast to the world. You can add pictures and videos along with your text, and you can share (retweet) other people's Tweets.

I always say that Facebook is for friends, and Twitter is for strangers.

You can't control who follows you on Twitter. You can only control who you follow. Other people can't post to your timeline, and you can mute someone whose Tweets you aren't interested in (but still want to follow, likely because they follow you...which begs the question, have they muted you, too?). Anything you say on Twitter can potentially be seen by anyone in the world.

It's perfect for writers in a lot of ways.

Once you have a book to sell, Twitter is a great way to get your message out. You can use hashtags (this # symbol, which makes the word that directly follows it searchable...for example, I frequently use #dinosaurs when Tweeting about my sci-fi novel so that anyone who decides to search Twitter for #dinosaurs will see my Tweet, in addition to everyone else's tweets about paleontology. It's a great way for dinosaur fans to find me and my book). You can connect with other writers (critical, especially if you don't have a local writing group and are looking for critique partners or beta readers). You can connect with fans and potential fans.

In the querying stage, you can (and should... no, must) follow agents. They don't have to be the agents you're specifically querying, but you'll be amazed at the insights you'll get reading what agents Tweet about all day. Many of them do a regular feature called #10queries or #querylunch where they will Tweet about...you guessed it...ten queries in a row. They can't say much in 140 characters, but you might see something like, "Q4 SF MG Cute concept but opens with infodump. Pass." This means it's the fourth query on their list at that moment. It's sci-fi, middle grade. They liked the idea, but it opened with too much world building and not enough story. They are sending a rejection to this author. Or you might see, "Q6 Rom Loved the feisty heroine. Strong writing. Full Request." So it's query six, it's a romance, and this lucky writer is about to get an email requesting their entire manuscript. You can start getting a feel for what agents are looking for, what catches their eye, what makes them request and what makes them pass. It's also a good way to remind yourself that you're not alone.

You'll also find the incredibly helpful #MSWL on Twitter. That stands for Manuscript Wish List, and it's a hashtag that agents and editors of small presses use to shout their wish lists to the world. If you search it and see that someone Tweeted that they're looking for non-traditional sci-fi erotica told from a female perspective, then you know exactly who to query with your zombie lesbian erotica novel.

A few more thoughts about Twitter.

Remember that this may be the first impression an agent or fan gets of you. They'll often scan your Twitter feed to see what you're about if they're interested in your manuscript. Make sure your handle is professional (@sexxymomma might be a fine handle if you're writing women's erotica, but not so much for a children's book author), and make sure your Tweets are something you'd be happy to share with them. Especially in the querying stage, consider keeping your political rants on the down low. Think of Twitter as part of your resume. You're looking for a job here. If you wouldn't want a potential employer to see it, don't put it on Twitter.

Start building your follower list right now. The best way to do that is to Tweet often, clever, and with hashtags. Are you writing a historical novel? Tweet about your research, #CivilWar. You'll quickly find a lot of other Civil War buffs who searched the hashtag and found you. If they follow you, then once you have a book to sell, they're a ready-made fan base.

Five Minutes to Success

Tweet about writing, and use #amwriting or #amediting. I get a few new followers every single time I do this, as fellow writers look up from their lonely cat-covered desks to find kindred spirits on the internet.

Mastering the Craft of Writing

Exercise: *Think About It*

Do you use Twitter regularly?

How could you start right now to build a following that will help you market your book when it's ready?

FIVE MINUTES TO SUCCESS

Time To Sell That Book!

Marketing Guidelines

You've worked so hard on your novel and it's finally out there in the world. If you're very lucky, you found an agent and a bigtime publisher who have chosen your book as a featured title. They'll be helping you market the book, and they have a huge network of professional reviewers and bookstore representatives who will help you along. But for most of us, marketing falls mostly on the author's shoulders. Even if you have a Big Five publisher, chances are that as a debut, they're not going to spend much on promoting your book. The days of nationwide book tours are over except for the very top-selling authors at the biggest publishers.

But if no one can find your book, no one will buy it.

We've talked a lot about making it good. We talked about social media and how you can start getting the word out long before the book is published.

So now what?

Your book is published. You're done, right? Just sit back and wait for the wheelbarrows of money to show up on your front porch?

Good luck with that.

Whether you self-publish or traditionally publish, most of your publicity is coming from you. Your publisher, if you have one, will help. They'll guide you on what to do (sometimes), but the actual DOING it is going to be up to you.

Authors hate marketing. Most of us would rather poke hot needles under our fingernails than ask our friends to buy our books. Many of us are introverts, and the thought of public speaking engagements makes us run for the bathroom. But we have to get over this if we want our books to succeed.

Remember how we talked about the millions of titles available on Amazon? Of course you do. And they're the problem. No matter what genre you write, there are hundreds of thousands of books already published in your genre. And more going up every single hour. No matter how good your book is, if no one knows about it, no one's going to buy it.

By now you should have set up an Amazon Author Page, a Facebook Author Page, a Twitter account, maybe an Instagram. You might have a blog, which can drive traffic if you do it well. And you're going to have to start talking about your book.

The marketing director at my publisher was super helpful to me in this stage. I didn't want to be "that author." You know the ones. They bombard you on Facebook and Twitter with the same message. *Buy My Book.* Over and over again. You've long since muted them, because that gets old fast. When my books release, I don't want anyone to get sick of hearing about them. I struggled with the idea of self-promotion. The marketing director put it this way: You wrote a book and you believe it's good, right? So what else do you think is good? What if you went to a restaurant and you had an amazing meal. Great food, great service. Would you tell people about it? Of course you would. You don't have a stake in the restaurant, but you want your friends to have good meals, too, right? And if they don't like dining out, that's okay. Marketing your book is no different. I never ask anyone to buy my books. But I want everyone to know that they exist. That way if something I've written appeals to them, or if they think it might make a good gift for someone they know, they'll know exactly where to go.

You have to believe in the quality of your product. You wouldn't tell your friends about an okay meal at an okay place. So your book has to be better than okay. If you don't believe it's worth their money, they won't believe it either.

In the next sections, we'll talk about specific things you can do to get the word out about your book so that no one has any excuse not to find it.

Exercise: *Think about it*

What do you think your biggest hurdle will be at marketing time?

Do you have ideas for a marketing plan yet?

Marketing Tools

You can buy a lot of stuff to publicize your book. Online sites like Vistaprint can help you create lots of marketing materials to get your brand out there. What's the best way to spend your money?

It depends on your market.

For my sci-fi and fantasy I love getting a booth at a convention. Comic-con, Sci-fi con, fantasy con... I do the big ones and the small. We'll talk specifically about cons in a later section, but for now let's talk about the stuff I buy.

Postcards and business cards are a must. I hand them out at cons, give them to people I meet, hang them on community cork boards, leave them at businesses that allow it. Keep them simple and make them useful. You need your book cover so it's recognizable, your name and some kind of contact info (Facebook page, blog, Twitter handle, email if you like), and a QR code that takes you right to the site where your book is sold. The easier you can make it for someone to make the purchase, the more likely it will happen. It's a lot easier to scan a QR code than it is to type your book title into a search bar, and sometimes that makes the difference. Get a thousand of them and hand them out anywhere you can.

If you do cons, signings, or personal appearances, a nice vinyl poster is essential. I get mine at Vistaprint because their software is easy to use and they're quite inexpensive. I put the book cover front and center, and depending on the cover, add quotes from great reviews around it. I always include my website on the poster. Various companies make stands that are light and portable so there's never a reason for you to be signing books without an impressive backdrop.

A lot of authors like to print out bookmarks and give them away. That's never something I've felt strongly about, because whenever I get them from other authors I immediately throw them away since I read almost exclusively on Kindle now. I don't think they're a bad idea, but I suspect they end up in the trash a lot more than they end up in books. If you have a local bookstore that would give them away on your behalf, that might make them more useful.

I also have three-fold brochures that I send to schools for bookings. We'll talk about school visits, but you must have some way of booking them, and a professional brochure is a good start.

A good media kit can also be useful. This is a document with a lot of eye-catching graphics that you can send to media outlets in hope of securing interviews or other public appearances. Your media kit should include your book cover, information about your book including genre, age group, and specific target audience (because if you have a book about dogs, they might want you for special dog-related events). Include your personal biographical information and at least one professional headshot (preferably the one that's on your book and all your branding). Include questions for interviews (because if you make their job easy, they're more likely to call), and a variety of ways to contact you. Send these to local news stations, radio stations, newspapers and blogs. Don't forget things like your college alumni magazine, and any professional organizations you belong to, especially if they have a magazine or newsletter.

One of my author friends has hired an artist to do renderings of her characters, and put them on RPG-style gaming cards which she gives out and sends as thank you gifts to beta readers. If your book is in a genre that supports this kind of thing, it might be worth doing.

We printed candy bar wrappers with our book covers on them and gave them away at a book fair to bloggers. I've seen a cookbook author who brought lots of little samples of his food to hand out, which drove sales nicely. A Native American author gave out scented bags of herbs. I hand out dinosaur stickers and little plastic dinosaurs to kids at conventions.

Mastering the Craft of Writing

Exercise: Think About...

... your genre and your specific manuscript: Is there a strong symbol or theme (like my plastic dinosaurs) that you could turn into an icon for your marketing?

If not, why not include a token (pick something easy to find and cheap to purchase) in your current work? What would it be?

What goes in your media kit?

Bookmarks or not? What would the design be?

Short Stories

You might not think about short stories as a potential marketing tool, but they're a great way to get your name out there. Having stories published not only helps in your bio section when you're querying, but it can help new readers find you.

Short stories have two basic markets: magazines and anthologies. Magazines tend to be genre-driven (science fiction magazines are the most common) and very specific in their guidelines. Anthologies are collections of short stories made into a book (e-book or physical). They're published by a variety of sources. Publishing houses do them, writing organizations do them, magazines do them. My publisher puts together collections of stories set in our authors' worlds, in the hope that if you're a fan of mine, you'll buy the anthology and find other Future House authors whose stories captivate you into buying their books.

I've been published in several anthologies with writers from all over the world. Anthologies expand your reach into the hands of many potential readers, and they're also really fun. Writing short stories is a great way to clear your mind after finishing a first draft before you start to edit, and you might as well make those stories earn their keep.

You can find anthologies looking for submissions by searching "anthology submission" online. Follow the guidelines they set out. If you submit a romance western story to an anthology looking for zombie horror, you're wasting your time (and theirs). Do not go above or below their word count restrictions. Don't think, "Oh, they said 3,000 words, but my story is really great so they'll be fine if it's 4500." No, they won't. They set restrictions for a reason. Follow the rules.

It's not necessary to stick to your own genre for short stories. I have several sci-fi stories published, one heart-wrenching dog story, and one steamy romance (my first publication). It's more helpful from a marketing standpoint to gain readers in the genre of your novel, but short stories are a great way to branch out and try new things. You're not committing to 80,000 words, so write whatever you want, and see where it takes you.

Some anthologies will have a professional editing process. Others expect your work to be in publishable form and won't do more than proofread. You probably won't know that until your work is accepted.

Once you've got a story in an anthology, you have something new to talk about on your social media, and something new to sell at personal appearances. I think of them like the cake tasting you do when you're getting married before you choose your wedding cake bakery. You want a little taste of the product you're going to buy and feed your guests. A short story can give readers a taste of your writing, and hopefully after trying it, they'll want the whole cake.

Five Minutes to Success

Exercise: Think About It

Do you have short stories lying around your hard drive that you could start putting to work?

Do you have an idea that wouldn't support a whole novel but might make a great short?

Is there a genre you've always wanted to try writing?

Cons, Schools, and Other Horrifying Events

If you write children's books, middle grade, or YA, you have an amazing opportunity to connect with your audience. Even the best teachers need a break now and then, and they love having outside speakers come in to entertain their minions for an hour. You can ask for a speaking fee if you're big time (although if you're that big, you're probably not reading this book), but here's how I do it. I don't charge a fee to come and do my presentation. But I do ask that two weeks before my visit, the students all receive an order form for my book (which my publisher offers at a discount for these events). On the day of the visit, I bring the books so that kids who have ordered them can get them signed and take them home. I earn money from book sales, and my books get into kids' hands. Plus, it's really fun.

Look, I'm not a kid person. I don't have any, and when people assume that I chose to write a middle grade dinosaur sci-fi adventure because I love kids, they're mistaken. I wrote for 40-something-year-old me who is still a twelve-year-old inside. So imagine my surprise when I did my first school visit and had an absolute blast.

Here's how you do it.

Start with a small school if you can, to get your feet wet. You probably know a teacher who'd be glad to have you. Prepare an interesting visit, which will depend on the age of the kids you're targeting, and the nature of your book. For young kids, don't prepare a speech, but plan an activity you can lead the kids in that matches something about your book. For middle graders, you can do a PowerPoint presentation, but it had better be interesting and involve a lot of participation. My current talk is aimed at fourth through sixth graders. It's called "What Makes a Hero," and it talks about the classic Hero's Journey using Star Wars as my example. We talk about heroes, real and fictional. We talk about the basic parts of a book using mine as an example (because... dinosaurs). Then we follow the Star Wars story with lots of film images and sounds. The talk lasts about forty minutes, I take questions, and do the signing.

High school kids have a longer attention span and can get much more in depth about the writing process. If you are an expert about your book's topic, you can base your talk about that (I could do a talk about dinosaurs instead of books). Try to work in questions that you can ask the kids to get them participating in your talk. And above all, don't be scared. If you're someone who hates public speaking, this is a great way to start getting over that fear. Remember that if all else fails and you're the worst speaker in history, these are kids who have gotten out of class to see you. They don't really care how uncomfortable you are because they're not in Algebra right now.

Conventions are another of my favorite ways to connect with readers. With my sci-fi and fantasy I do Comic-cons and fantasy cons. You can pay for a vendor booth and set up your display, and the cost will depend on how big the con is. The big Comic Expo in Cincinnati draws over 30,000 attendees, and the table costs a couple hundred bucks.

Put together a nice display. You'll want a tablecloth, a banner to hang behind you, stands for your books, and whatever other decorations fit your theme. I always put out a bowl of candy. This is where I'll give out a thousand postcards in a weekend (with my book cover and a QR code on the back for easy buying). And it's where I'll get to tell people about my book. Have a 30-second speech ready, but don't memorize a script because you'll sound like an idiot. Don't be too aggressive, and just be a normal person. If you open with, "Do you want to buy my book?" you'll get a lot of hasty retreats. I usually lead with, "So what do you like to read?" and then have a conversation. Sometimes my books will be a good fit. Other times they won't. Sometimes they'll buy one for a family member if it's not their taste but we had a connection. It's all about being a real person and having a normal conversation. If you're being a salesman, you'll drive people away. Just talk to people.

Wear comfortable shoes and bring a small rug or foam mat to stand on because you'll be standing all weekend. Don't retreat to the back of your booth and play with your phone. Do make friends with the vendors around you. Always have a notebook and pen on the front of your table and encourage people to sign up for your mailing list.

Many cons have presentations all day, and this is a great time to pull out your PowerPoint again. This book came from the presentation Jeri and I concocted called, "What's Next After the First Draft?" which we give at conventions whenever we can. Some smaller cons will give you a discount on your booth rental in exchange for you putting on workshops or lectures. So think about what you can offer. It doesn't have to be about writing. It should be applicable to the con's theme. Sometimes there are author or expert panels you can sit on. And don't forget to invite everyone who comes to your presentation to come on down to the vendors' hall and chat after the program. This is a great time to network with other writers and build your audience.

Book clubs love having authors come to talk about their books. Even if it's a smaller club, those are still sales, and still people talking about your book.

Libraries sometimes host speakers, and if your book has a specific theme, there might be groups who would love to hear from you (like gardening clubs if you write about horticulture). Be creative and find the people who might be interested in reading your story.

Exercise: Think About It

What kinds of events would be appropriate for you to sell your books?

What topics could you prepare a presentation about, and what groups of people would be interested in that presentation?

Five Minutes to Success

Blogging for Success and Mailing List Musts

You've started a website and blog, right? You're building readers a few at a time by providing interesting content at regular intervals? No?

Uh oh.

Look, not everyone is suited for a blog. But they're a great way to connect with potential readers, and your blog does not have to be about writing. Let me repeat that. It doesn't have to be about writing.

It helps if your blog is about something that has to do with your book. It would be great if I had a dinosaur blog where I talked about paleontology news and dino-facts. But I don't. I should. I might someday, but right now my blog is a work in progress, and that's okay. The important thing is that it exists.

Update your blog regularly, and give people a reason to check it out. Provide them something useful. Pet tips. Recipes. Restaurant reviews. It doesn't really matter what it is, just that it's there and if people search for "Best Mexican food in Detroit" they'll find your blog, which will be full of helpful information and a sidebar with links to Buy My Books.

Blogging about a topic people search for is just good publicity. Get people to read your words, no matter what those words are about. Hook them with your writing style and they'll want to read more.

Lists are great for popping up in search engines. A blog entry about your favorite enchilada recipe is good, but if it's called something like "Top 10 Best Easy Mexican CrockPot Meals" you'll get hits when people search for Mexican food, easy recipes, and slow cooker meals.

The more followers your blog attracts, the more potential readers will be ready and waiting for your next book, even if it has nothing to do with enchiladas.

And your blog is a great place to have a sign up for your mailing list.

Don't have a mailing list?

Uh oh.

There are several easy ways to set one up. I use MailChimp. They make it easy to import emails (which you'll get through your blog and at personal appearances) and can do it automatically from your blog when people want to sign up.

This is a great trust. Do not abuse it.

I've signed up for people's email lists before, and they've spammed me twice a week. I unsubscribe as soon as I realize that's their pattern. For my own purposes, I send a mailing when I have something interesting to say. New publications, news about an upcoming event, a contest or some other news I want to share. I never email more than once a month. The people who have given me their addresses deserve respect for that gift. And they're valuable to me. These are people who have had interest in my work. They're my readers. They're the people I want to be sure know about my latest publication.

Build your list and take care of it.

Exercise: ***Think About It***

What topics could you blog about?

How often can you commit to writing a blog post to keep your readers engaged?

Reviews: Why They Matter and How to Get Them

There's an internet meme out there with a list of free ways you can support an artist. Talk about their work, share their work, review their work. I share this post whenever it comes across my timeline because it's so important. Reviews can make or break you.

Do you shop online? Of course you do. And when you do, how do you decide what product you're going to buy? Brand name, product specifications, and reviews. If you're deciding between two items and one has two stars and the other has five, which are you going to choose? Whether it's a light for the top of your flagpole or your next read, an unbiased review often makes the difference in what you choose to purchase.

Obviously you want lots of good reviews for your book. The big bestsellers get tens of thousands, but if you're published on Amazon, the key number is fifty. Once your book gets fifty reviews (no matter how many stars each one gives you), you get put into their double-secret algorithm and they will start promoting you. You know how if you buy a book in a certain genre, you'll get a list of other books they recommend based on what you just bought? Yeah, fifty reviews is how your book can get on that list. And Amazon loves to send out emails..."Based on your recent purchase, we thought you'd like..."and here's another place where your book can be recommended to someone who bought another book in your genre. This is how buzz begins.

So you need reviews, and you need them fast. Assuming you're making a big deal of your launch day (on your website, social media, mailing list, and anywhere else you can shout that you've got a book coming out), that's the day the most people are likely to hear about your book. They're most likely to go to your page and consider it right then. How does it look if they go and there aren't any reviews? It looks like no one has bought it. So why would they? How does it look if there are already thirty or forty good reviews on the very first day? Now that's a book they might buy.

How do you get first day reviews?

ARCs.

ARC stands for Advance Review Copy. Your publisher will (should) make these available, and if you're self-pubbing you can do it yourself. The ARC is (usually) a digital download of the manuscript. It might be pre-proofread and include a disclaimer that typos could be present. That's because you need to get your ARCs out to your advance review readers early enough that they can read it and have a review ready for day one.

ARCs are free. You might twitch at that, thinking, "But Wendy, why would I give my book away free? These are people who would buy it and I need sales." Yes, you need sales. But to get sales you need reviews, and you need them right now. Those of your ARC readers who are friends and family will buy it anyway, and if some people don't, it's not a big deal. Think big picture. Think about how this free copy could turn into a positive review that could turn into another sale. Or two. Or ten. Or a hundred. Trust me, free ARCs will make you money in the long run.

No matter how well-intentioned your friends are, you have to assume that you'll get a return of about one in three reviews for the ARCs you send out. People just get busy and forget. You should send out two or three times as many ARCs as you want reviews (remembering the magic fifty Amazon reviews), and send two email reminders to everyone who has one. The first reminder should go out a couple of weeks before launch day, saying something like, "Hope you're enjoying the book. Thanks so much for reading, and don't forget to write a review in advance so you can post it for me on launch day!" Then the day before launch send another one that reminds them to post the review tomorrow. Don't be upset with people who don't follow through, just move on.

So where do you find these people?

Unlike Beta readers who should be knowledgeable about writing, ARC reviewers can be anyone. Friends, family, coworkers. Anyone you trust to do what they say they'll do. You can put out a call on your Facebook page, and in any writing groups you belong to. Social groups, office email, mom's bridge club...doesn't matter. Find people. Don't send unsolicited ARCs, but try to get as many readers as you can. All you need is their email.

Book bloggers and podcasters are great ARC readers. They love to see something before the rest of the world gets it, and an ARC might turn into an interview on their site.

While you're at it, dream big. In addition to readers and bloggers, choose a few bigger name writers in your genre. If you can find their email, ask them if they'd consider reading an ARC and offering a blurb for you to use in your marketing. You might be surprised who's happy to reach down the ladder and help a new writer get a leg up. The worst they can say is no, which they won't, because if the answer is no you'll just never hear back from them.

Five Minutes to Success

Exercise: Think About It

How many people can you count on to read your book and offer you a review on launch day? Make a list of their names. Talk to them ahead of time.

Should you be joining some on-topic social or online groups right now so you have a bigger pool of potential ARC readers when you need them?

Don't be a Jerk

If there's one rule for interacting with the public, that's it. Be nice. All the time. Whether you're meeting readers in person or interacting with them online, don't be a jerk. It will come back to bite you.

There will always be trolls. Some people live to poop on other people's dreams. They'll harass you online, they'll give you bad reviews, they'll try to get a rise out of you because that's what they do. Do not take their bait. Ignore them and move on. They'll find a more interesting target soon enough.

Remember that your online persona is all most readers will know of you. Getting into flame wars about politics or religion might seem like a great idea, but never forget that the internet is forever. Tweets you send today will still exist in ten years, and someone will find them.

Avoid the hard sell. If I find you on Twitter and of your last ten tweets, nine of them are some version of "Buy My Book!" I will never follow you. Or if I'm following because you followed me, I'll mute you instantly. If there's nothing on your author Facebook page except Buy My Book, I won't do it.

Be a real person. Be a nice person. Be a person I'd want to hang out with for six or eight hours, because in asking me to read your novel, that's what you're really asking.

Be available. Be easy to find. Readers want to connect with you. They want to know about you as a person, so don't make it impossible for them to find you. Always be polite and never get drawn into an argument even if you're right and they're totally wrong.

You're an author now. That's a public figure. You might never be a household name celebrity, but once you have a published novel, you're not just "Joe who runs the tire store" anymore. Be professional and courteous and know that you represent us all in your dealings with the public.

Exercise: **Think About It**

How will you respond to unkind remarks about your work online?

End Notes

The title of this book is *Five Minutes to Success*. We intended it to serve as a series of five-minute lessons to help you improve your writing, learn to edit, and understand the basics of the current publishing world.

I'm sure you figured out that it takes a lot more than five minutes.

The best writers make it look so easy. But the best writers have a lot of help. You don't read Stephen King's first drafts. You don't read his second or his third. By the time one of his novels hits the shelf, it's gone through multiple rewrites, agent feedback, more rewrites, and at least three editors. The book you pick up off the shelf is a finished, polished work, and it's why you know exactly what you're getting when you open a novel with his name on it.

That's what we want for you.

Guaranteed quality.

We want everyone who picks up your books to say, "Gee, here's another book by that author I like so much. They're always great, so please take my money."

After reading this workbook and doing the exercises you should be well on your way to crafting a solid, saleable novel. If you've realized specific areas where you need more help, now you know where to concentrate to improve your craft.

We hope you've had some fun and learned some skills. If you enjoyed this book, please drop us a line. We'd love to hear your success stories.

And remember that part about how reviews help authors sell books? Yeah, it's time for that. Just a sentence and a couple of stars would really make a difference.

Now get back to work. You've got writing to do.

Five Minutes to Success

About the Authors

It may seem funny to buy a book about writing from two writers you have maybe never heard of. Shouldn't you be getting your advice from New York Times bestselling authors and the agents that are getting million-dollar movie deals?

Yes, you probably should. But most of them aren't writing books like this. They're too busy writing New York Times bestsellers and making millions of dollars.

The advice we have given you in this book has been hard-won, earned through mistakes and successes over many years in the writing game. We've had triumphs and tragedies, and we're figuring out this brave new world of e-books and book blogs and social media buzz right alongside you. We're not so far ahead of you that we've forgotten how we got here.

I'm Jeri Fay Maynard, the author of three Young Adult novels: *Panda Girl*, *Red Kicks*, *4 Winds*, and one Literary novel called *The Wilding Days*. Currently all my books are out of print, but *Panda Girl* will be back in circulation asap. I'm a screenwriter, comic book writer, and have a historical mid-grade novel in search of a publishing home. I facilitate a Screenwriter's Group in Cincinnati and teach writing workshop/classes for all ages. The secret thing about me is that I love LOVE Asian media (all kinds) and am always up for a road trip. Wanna' go?

You can check out Jeri Fay Maynard at FB.com/jerjonji

Five Minutes to Success

I'm D. W. Vogel, author of *Horizon Alpha: Predators of Eden*, *Horizon Alpha: Transport Seventeen*, and *Flamewalker*, along with numerous published short stories. I have an agent and a traditional publisher, and I work as a freelance editor. I'm currently the president of Cincinnati Fiction Writers, and in my spare time I'm a veterinarian, which doesn't make me qualified to write a book on writing, but does mean that I'm handy with a scalpel (for cutting unwanted testicles off your dog, or useless words from your manuscript).

You can check out D.W. Vogel at FB.com/dwvogel

Made in the USA
Columbia, SC
25 March 2019